Flying M

Edward Maixner

graphics by Ed & Betsy Maixner

and Walter P. Jacobs

Cover photo: *East Rainy Butte, south of the former Maixner farmstead. (Photo by Elizabeth Gardner Luzar)*

Title page photo: *Ed on his Tractall, a prized fourth Christmas (1951) gift. It was pricey, considering my parents' tight budget. But farm markets were kind that year. North Dakota spring wheat prices had been running a robust $2 and more per bushel, and feeder calf prices soared to $32-$34 per hundredweight in 1951. What's more, I wore out a catalog page and Mom's ears promoting the attributes of that toy tractor. So, lucky me!*

Printed by CreateSpace

ISBN: 978-1548304362

Copyright © 2017 Edward Maixner

Author's Note

This is my memoir of growing up in Rainy Butte Township, Slope County, North Dakota. My childhood there on a serene patch of America's Northern Plains is a gift for which I am ever grateful.

Though I sought available historical and news records to compile this book, my telling is more than a half-century after the fact. So, no doubt, it contains distortions and lapses of memory. Some of the humor, especially, is surely embellished in the retelling. Still, I try to be faithful to what I and others recall about those years on our family farm and in my hometown.

One might expect that reporting on something as straightforward as one's own childhood would be a solo project. It was not. My brothers, sisters, cousins and others helped add tales, corrections, and historical facts about the farm and local history. I salute my wife Betsy for her help in taking photos and formatting graphics; author and fellow journalist Patricia McNeely for coaching a fledgling self-publisher on format and logistics; my brother Rick for reading my draft chapters and helping to correct errors and add details; veteran author and journalist Henry Schulte for a complimentary copy editing, and my late uncle, Walt Jacobs, for the use of his Rainy-Buttes-ambiance drawings, including the one below.

Writing in nearby Lemmon, S.D., years ago, author Kathleen Norris observed, "the Plains are full of 'good telling stories,' and while our sense of being forgotten . . . makes it all the more important that we preserve them and pass them on, instead we often neglect them." So my book is in part an offering against that neglect and is a gift to my family, friends, people of my hometown, western North Dakota and others who may enjoy this sort of narrated scrapbook about growing up on a farm and ranch in the 1950s and 1960s.

The Flying M family gets under way

In front, Joe and infant Laura Lu; the others from left are Frank, Dad, Fran, Rick, Bill, Mom, and yours truly (fall 1952); Daria, yet to arrive.

Contents

Introduction	9
Flying M Family	12
The Neighborhood	17
The Rainy Buttes	21
Our Field and Garden Crops	27
Flying M Critters	31
Wildlife	39
Yay for Electricity and Mechanical Innovation!	43
Farm Jobs & Discovery	49
Mom & the Flying M Kitchen	55
Grandma Luella	59
A Throng of Teachers, Young and Old	63
Home Town	71
School Days	77
A Dark Character Called 'Big Dad'	85
Trips & Vacations	91

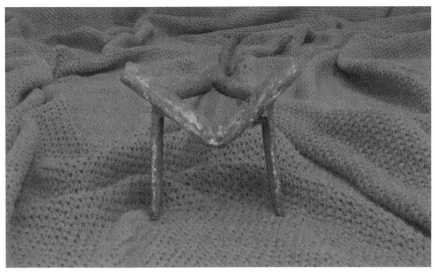

A blowtorch heated our branding iron to a red glow on fall roundup day. (Photo is compliments of Jack Maixner, who keeps this Flying M souvenir.)

Introduction

Most people who have not seen how a hail storm on the Northern Plains can pound fields of ripening crops to the ground can surely imagine what a disaster that event can spell for a farmer who has nursed his crops from seeds to thriving plants and depends on those crops to pay the costs of family living. Hail seemed to take a toll every year on every farm in our area, including ours. One summer around 1960, we got a doozy. We lit holy candles, as many Catholic families did when storm clouds were building to our west or northwest, and we said a rosary if we could gather at home in time to do so. My parents knew full well of the field and financial havoc that approached, and we sat around our big table in our country kitchen as the tempest began to take its toll.

For a few years, Dad joined other Slope County farmers to pay cooperatively for airplanes to "cloud seed," spreading silver iodide dust in front of the approaching thunderheads to make droplets condense quicker and fall as rain, rather than staying aloft to accumulate layer upon layer of ice and form large hail stones. Many farmers hoped and believed in that trick. Dad did also. He was impressed that the cloud seeding at least substantially reduced the numbers and size of stones if the pilots could get in position fast enough to do their work. But if the silver iodide does work, it didn't work that day.

Mom cried when the hail battered our house. Not loudly, but there were tears. Dad didn't feel a lot better, I am sure. But when the storm had passed, he went around to the back of the house and filled a big bucket from the hailstones that had banked up against the foundation. We had sweet cream in the fridge from our motley roster of milk cows. And we had sugar. So, he said, "I guess we may as well make some ice cream." Which we did. It appeared that my parents enjoyed the treat as much as the rest of us, perhaps because they wanted to prove to themselves they could. Perhaps to show us and remind themselves that our lives did not end with a damned hail storm.

This book is about growing up in the 1950s and 1960s in a big family on an average-sized farm and ranch in southwestern North Dakota and in New England, my nearby home town. My parents, Richard (Dick) Donald Maixner and Laura Hazel Steckman Maixner, just called their place a farm, but my brothers dubbed it officially the Flying M Ranch when they began farming there in 1970 and 1971.

My years there, like the hailstone ice cream, were so often fun because we made it such. The time and place suggest a plain-and-simple rural American life. That is pretty much how I viewed it at the time. The place was tranquil, though saying that may seem to belie the reality of a working farm full of animals, motorized machines and a gaggle of kids. So, kind of ironically, it seems, my childhood was plain and simple within the scope of the Flying M but as wonderfully unusual as I thought it was ordinary at the time.

I've called the place both a ranch and a farm. Which is it? Ranching is a type of farming done primarily to raise animals – cattle, sheep, goats, bison, horses and more – that graze in pastures during the warmer months and eat hay and/or grain in winter when the pastures are dormant. We did that, so our farm was a ranch. But it was more generally a diversified farm because we also grew a myriad of crops, had a few pigs, hundreds of chickens and a dozen or so turkeys for meat, plus several dozen hens for laying eggs, and other animals.

Though Flying M Ranch was perhaps a catchy name for our grain and livestock farm, it was an official name. Dad listed the brand in the North Dakota Stockmen's Association brands registry, and it was used to identify our cattle. It was not chosen at random. My uncle Stan Maixner, Dad's younger brother, was a navigator and bombardier in a B-24 Liberator on the World War II European front. He fashioned his own Flying 8 (an 8 with wings) brand to salute the U.S. Army 8th Air Force, in which he had served. So Dad followed suit with a winged M for his brand. Because cattle are costly animals to lose, ranchers branded them so they could be readily reclaimed if they escaped their pasture and joined neighboring herds, or if they were rustled (stolen).

Americans often think of ranches in the shoot'em-up tradition of 20th Century Old West movies or the dude ranches or sprawling spreads of wealthy folks, many of whom like to show off their wealth but know little about farming. In the view of my parents, such showy ranchers were called "all hat" (nothing inside it), so they preferred to call themselves farmers.

When brothers Bill, Rick and Joe started farming in the early 1970s, with farm operations all based at the rapidly expanding Flying M farmstead, they attached a "Flying M Ranch" nameplate to Dad's mailbox. Years later, Rick wrote a poem about Dad, and this was the first verse:

He never called himself a rancher;

never bragged about his spread.

Talked about his wheat crop;

bragged about his kids instead.

He never owned a pair of Levi's;

didn't wear those pointy shoes.

Wore solid engineer's boots with his Big Mac blues.

(Note: Big Mac has long been JC Penney's low-cost workman's jeans.)

Flying M Family

Mom did supply Dad with a pair or two of Levi jeans. They had a trimmer fit than Big Macs and cost more, and he would wear them for some trips and other events off the farm. Besides, she took pride in the way we all looked, and we were hardly impoverished. But Rick's poem was true to Dad's unpretentious character. He loved jokes and a good laugh when it was story telling time, but had no liking for ostentatious or arrogant people. He was a Farmers Union member to the core, highly valuing the strength of farmers getting together for political impact and co-op marketing. That approach began right at home: Two brothers and brother-in-law Walt Jacobs all farmed within 15 miles of each other. They frequently lent each other farm machinery, tractors, and/or their own labor to reduce the need for capital expenditures and to farm efficiently. Dad often did the same with neighboring farmers.

Most of us pick up our style of humor from the folks we grow up with, and I believe I'm a Flying M product in my own preferences. Here are samples of my parents' humor. Ladies first. Mom finished two years at Dickinson State Teachers College (now Dickinson State University), sufficient to secure a teaching certificate and teach high school kids in small towns, eventually taking a job in New England and boarding at the Gardner Hotel. Dad was in his late twenties, doing resident services and maintenance at the hotel. That's how my parents met.

Mom's humor tended to tales of misadventure – goofy misstatements and missteps that people make. The school teacher, she relished malapropisms. Several in our township farming area were first generation Germans from the Black Sea region of Russia, or from Norway, so they were fountains of misstatements. She enjoyed a neighboring farmer complimenting her Hilex (lilac) bushes, and his news that another elderly neighbor was having prospect (prostate) problems. Once, sitting in a Dickinson clinic waiting room, a German lady from Russia greeted the physician as he crossed the waiting room: "Doctor, I came for you to taste (test) my urine."

Dad, on the other hand, liked tall tales, funny political one-liners, and kidding people about politics. He had a pack of calling cards printed up; a copy of one is pasted at right. Many of his conservative relations and close friends were treated to his card.

In his 1948 run for re-election, President Harry Truman did a whistle-stop tour on a Northern Pacific train across the West. Dad retold a Truman line for years, delivered when he, Stan Maixner and Walt Jacobs drove about 220 miles north to Minot, which was on the Great Northern Railroad (now part of BNSF) route, to catch Truman's brief stop there. In Washington State, supporters had been yelling the campaign mantra, "Give 'em hell, Harry," and

Truman replied: "Aw, I don't give 'em hell, I just tell the truth about 'em and they think it's hell." So Dad heard him deliver that same line in Minot. Truman got good laughs with that one through election day.

Maurice O'Connell, owner of the local Citizens State Bank, was one of Dad's best friends. He liked to pose this puzzler to others, but especially to Maurice: "A banker has a glass eye; how can you tell which is the glass one?" Then he would supply the answer: "If you look closely, you may see a bit of warmth and humanity in the glass one." [Very sadly, in 1983, many years after I left the farm, Maurice and his wife, Kathleen, and two others were executed by shotgun blasts from an estranged husband of one of his bank's staff whom O'Connells were trying to help.]

Dad also got a big charge out of outbursts by Martha Clendenen, who owned and operated the only bar in Amidon, our population-impaired county seat. Her crusty, blunt declarations and unbridled responses to patrons made her an Amidon icon. She once contracted for some refurbishing of her bar's front and interior, and, in appreciation, the contractors sent bouquets for her tables at her grand reopening. Dad complimented Martha on the pretty flowers. She responded: "Flowers! Whoever heard of flowers in a goddamn bar?"

My parents themselves, of course, came from somewhere. Both were from rural North Dakota households modeled by can-do attitudes of self-reliance, creativity and resourcefulness, and that is the way they approached life. Owing to fate, my grandfathers didn't loom so large in my life in a direct way. Vendelin Maixner was born in Bohemia and took the name of John in America. He died two months after my first birthday, felled by strokes. Mom's father, George Steckman, died when I was 10 years old. He and Grandma Flossie lived in Bismarck, which in those years was more than three hours' drive from the Flying M, so I saw them only occasionally. They took Joe and me fishing a couple of times. The point is, though, that my grandfathers, who died too young, and my grandmothers, who both lived into my adult years, helped shape how my parents and I viewed work and lived on the ranch.

George Steckman married Flossie Gage in 1914 and they settled in Tappen, a little town an hour east of Bismarck. He owned and ran a pool hall, broke wild horses in his corral at the edge of town, organized and promoted rodeos and boxing matches, and even managed a few boxers, too. He was the town cop as well. Among other things, his strong tenor singing voice was also in demand for solos at formal and community events.

They later moved to Bismarck, where he was hired as a guard at the North Dakota State Penitentiary. An escaping inmate once beat him with a steel bar to within an inch of his life. But he healed and in time rose to the deputy warden position. He also refurbished cars in his garage for resale. Flossie was an industrious homemaker, non-stop gardener, canner, baker, etc. After raising her own five kids, she helped raise three of her granddaughters after her oldest daughter, Marie, lost her husband as a young mom and had to work full-time.

John Maixner and Luella Langer Maixner married in Owatonna, MN, in 1906. In the spring of that year, John filed his homestead claim in Hume Township, north of Scranton, ND, about 15 miles from where my parents later farmed. Like so many others around them, starting a farm on the isolated prairies forced them to be inventive and self-reliant. John went by horse-drawn wagon about 30 miles north to Belfield, located on the Northern Pacific Railroad route, to pick up a load of lumber for building his barn and retrieve Luella and their first-born daughter, Rosella, in the same trip. That was Luella's introduction to southwestern North Dakota and their farm.

Luella gave birth to Van, their first son, by herself, except for her toddler daughter at home with her. John was meeting with area farmers to organize the first township school district, and he picked up a neighbor lady, Mrs. Peterson, who gave Luella some midwife assistance shortly after Van entered this world. Oral family history has it that Mrs. Peterson put John to task immediately boiling dish towels for her, and that the towel boiling was mostly to keep him busy and out of the way.

Family members often spoke of the couple's resourcefulness. Luella raised a flock of turkeys each year. Some were eaten at their own table, but most were sold, providing Luella cash to send Dad's younger siblings to St. Mary's High School in New England. I remember the gravity flow water supply system that ran from a single well near their barn: Water was pumped fresh and cold for use in the milk parlor and into a large tank just outside the barn for dairy cows, beef cattle and horses to drink but also to cool cans of fresh milk and cream, which were set down in a section of the tank separated from the cattle. Then, the overflow from the tank was channeled down to Luella's big garden, which stretched beyond the livestock watering paddock.

Let's meet the Flying M siblings (see photo on page 4). There were eight of us, same as the number of planets (since Pluto was demoted to dwarf status). First, Bill and Rick. I was third rock from the Sun, so to speak. Then Joe (formally, Joel), twins Frances (Dakotah) and Frank, then Laura Lu and Daria (Darcy).

Leon Wandler

We also gained an older foster brother, Leon Wandler, who was living with us much of the time when I was a toddler and preschooler. Leon was a cousin whose mother, Rosella Maixner Wandler, died in 1938 in Spokane, Wash., leaving seven kids and a dad who was not equipped to raise them. Grandma Luella Maixner, and Stan, who was still single, went west to retrieve the Wandler siblings and brought them to the farm to raise them. John and Luella took the situation into hand and assigned the older ones among their offsprings' households. My parents were awarded Leon; he was 10 years older than Bill, my oldest brother, and 15 years older than me. He was handsome, gentle and endeared by our family. He was also very adept mechanically and had a knack for trade skills generally, so my older brothers and I learned a lot of things from Leon. He went to machinist school and worked on our farm in summers, but then went for a hitch in the U.S. Army, and so I saw him less frequently once I was into the primary grades and beyond.

Nonetheless, I can still see Leon throwing a lit cigarette into a pan of gasoline just outside the front door of the farm shop. I knew that gasoline is very volatile and flammable, so I was shocked when the cigarette stub simply went pfft and drowned in the fuel. While a lit match, with its head of red phosphorus and sulfur, immediately ignite gasoline fuel or fumes, Leon explained to me at age five that a smoldering cigarette's temperature is lower than gasoline's ignition temperature, and so the fuel just extinguishes the burning ash.

Although the match didn't ignite the pan of gasoline, it wasn't often quiet on our farmstead for very long at any one time. What with the family, Beauty, the quarter horse, the dog and always a bevy of cats, plus herds and flocks of farm animals to attend to, within any few minutes in a summer day you might see and hear all sorts of things: A truck arriving with a load of hay to be stacked; a tractor with an attached disk cultivator roaring out of the yard to kill weeds in a corn field or one of the previous year's wheat fields; a Farmers Union Oil Co. fuel truck rumbling in with a blast of its horn on the way to refill the gasoline or diesel fuel bulk tanks down by the farm shop; a neighbor or uncle stopping in to consult with Dad or borrow something from the shop; a Hereford cow bawling at her calf who's frolicking just outside the pasture fence. Just then, a gust of wind might accelerate the big fan on the windmill that pumped water into a big, round open tank for cattle and other farm use, making its pump rod click, click, click against the tower's frame. Perhaps a cat fight as well. And our dog, Buck, was always alert to his task of announcing all arrivals and promptly chasing all available cats into refuges beneath trucks and farm buildings, ensuring he got any available people strokes and reminding the cats of their rank.

In the fall of 1955, when I was eight years old, we moved into a new house on the farmstead. Here is a short telling of it. We moved out of a small old house that was atop a hill on the farmstead my parents bought in 1946. We put beds, dressers, clothing, dishes and a few other loads of essentials into the open box on the farm truck and moved across the yard to the waiting rambler. It had been built since the previous winter by Dad, local carpenter Frank Heick and a revolving team of other local tradesmen, family and friends. Pat Weisgerber, a high school vocational education teacher and friend of my parents, supervised the electrical wiring. Vets (Sylvester) Zeren and Willy Fitterer and perhaps others with Gardner & Zeren, the New England hardware store, installed plumbing and heating systems. The house had just two bedrooms on the mail floor. In the basement, five beds and dressers were lined up along one side of the unfinished, cement-block-walled lower level. With a shower-and-toilet area enclosed by another cement block wall in one corner, the basement became the boys' dorm. Basement bedrooms were built for us a few years later, with knotty pine walls, closets and drawers.

With two parents and eight children in the same house, I suppose a paragraph should be included about discipline, since that many kids running about spells opportunity for a lot of mischief. The Maixner kids knew well who the bosses were, and my parents didn't like hitting or spanking us, so physical punishments were not frequent. Dad hit me perhaps twice in my life, and Mom bought a "Fanny Whacker" (see photo), which hung on a wall above our kitchen table. Perhaps she got it as a gift. It bore funny doggerel about its intended use on misbehaving spouses, kids, dogs and so forth. Mom fairly often threatened use of the whacker, but it seldom came off the wall. Dad didn't bother with the whacker; his condemnation of behavior was the last thing anyone in our household wanted to hear.

Fanny Whacker often drew comments but wasn't used often on our butts.

The Neighborhood

View of Baldy Butte, left, and West Rainy Butte from our farmstead hilltop

We lived in Slope County, which had the fewest people among North Dakota counties, averaging just three people in each two square miles. Today, fewer than half as many live there. Our part of the county was Rainy Butte Township, a square six miles long on each side (36 square miles); no town or village. But the township was on the east side of the county, near the town of New England, which is in Hettinger County. The first European settlers had arrived in Rainy Butte Township to farm and raise cattle only a half-century earlier.

Dozens of small farms and ranches were scattered across the township. The dwellers included old bachelors and widowers, including some who had homesteaded near the start of the 20th Century. Most were members of Catholic and protestant congregations in nearby New England or Lutheran churches out in Slope and Hettinger counties. Most of our shopping and other business was done in New England or Dickinson, a much larger town a half-hour farther north from New England by highway.

Rainy Butte Township changed a lot from my birth in 1947 through my college years in the late 1960s and my brothers' start in farming in the early 1970s. Small farms disappeared as old timers died off or retired and their farmland was added to larger, expanding farms. Thus, while total farmland acreage changed little, the number of farms shrank, and the distance between farmsteads increased. In the U.S., the number plunged from 5.4 million in 1950 to 2.3 million in 1974, a shrinkage of 57 percent. Our township followed suit, and my family was part of the trend. Dad bought land and expanded moderately during about 30 years of farming; my brothers did likewise through their 20 years or so of farm operations.

Over a period of years, for example, Dad bought quarter-sections of land from two farmers who retired and another half-section from the surviving sister of another old timer who died on his farm. He also rented one quarter that his brother Albert had purchased a few miles from his own homestead. Those additions left him as an average size farm for our area, because other farmers were expanding similarly.

Still, despite the continued farmer exodus via deaths and retirements, our township was far from deserted when I lived there. On average, there still remained an occupied farmstead along each half-mile or mile of highway or graded road in our part of the township.

One outcome of farm consolidations was the proliferation of abandoned schoolhouses. Improved roads made school bus service easier and, with a steady decline in family size and the continued thinning of population of school-aged kids on farms, the county closed a lot of country schools and bused kids instead to consolidated schools in nearby towns. We kept one school house in usable shape to serve as our township precinct polling place. Another one left crumbling near one of our tracts was mostly a home for rodents. However, I still own a 1946 vinyl-backed pull-down map of North Dakota that I rescued from that schoolhouse.

With Slope County handling the public schools, the main responsibility left for the township was its roads. The township's first graded and graveled roads, except for a section of two-lane Highway 21 along its north edge, were being planned and built when I was in the primary grades. I recall their arrival. First, the sod alongside our flat trails was sort of plowed up toward the road center by a grader with a sort of conveyer belt. The machine was called a mucker, and after several passes a high road was roughly formed. Bulldozers and front-end loaders were used to open channels for culverts and bridges. A grader leveled the road top and the gravel, leaving us with roads fit for driving in all but serious downpours or blizzards. That improvement, coming when I was eight years old and brother Bill old enough to secure a restricted driver's license, allowed all the school-aged Maixners to start commuting to school daily, rather than boarding at St. Mary's School. Rainy Butte Township landowners no doubt paid a robust assessment for the cost of their new roads. What I recall most about township road and bridge maintenance, once they were built, was its simplicity. It was grass roots government at its basics. To care for the roads in our part of the township, a little grader, called a maintainer, waited in our farm yard. Originally made to be pulled by either horses or tractor, one could swing its 12-foot road-leveling blade to the desired angle and lock it in place and spin one of two spoked wheels to control the height of the blade's right and left ends. If our roads became rutted by traffic in muddy spring conditions, or when traffic had pushed too much gravel to the edge of the road, we hooked the maintainer to a farm tractor and went out maintaining, providing a smoother path and sweeping the gravel back into the driving lanes.

Also, when the timbers in a township bridge became rotten or broken, the township officers would order new timbers and spikes and haul or have them dropped at the site. Then volunteers would gather at the site. One of us would bring a tractor with hydraulic hoist to lift and position the planks, and we would team up to replace timbers or a whole bridge deck.

In my earliest years, Rainy Butte Township had its own precinct, located along Highway 21 on the route to New England. I visited the building occasionally when my parents voted. Rainy Butte Precinct voters later cast their ballots at the orphaned Moord (also called Gatske) school house. Its days as a school had ended, but it was kept in functional condition by the township. There was a supply of firewood and/or coal for heating, so it could serve as an occasional meeting and polling place.

Our township road grader looked just like the one shown here. (Photo is compliments of Jack Nitz & Assoc., Fremont, NE)

Unfortunately, I never did get to walk into either of those polling places and vote. At the time, the right to vote started at age 21, and I was already 23 years old when the 26th Amendment to the U.S. Constitution, lowering the voting age to 18 years, was approved in 1971. So the only vote that I cast in Slope County was by absentee ballot. I was 21 years old in October 1968 and a senior at North Dakota State University when that year's national elections occurred. Thus, my absentee ballot was mailed to my county and sent to the precinct for recording.

In many ways, the Gatske schoolhouse was not different than perhaps thousands of rural polling places during my childhood. It was a group project involving more than just the poll judges and clerks policing the ballots. One or more election officials arrived early to fire up the stove and heat the place, and, for years, a farmer brought his tractor and portable power generator to run lights in the building. Voting booths were just board shelves cordoned off by blankets hung across corners. For the poll officials, twelve or more hours of waiting for often fewer than 100 people to show up to vote meant a lot of slack time. So most of the action was just visiting or playing pinochle and/or whist at a table or two in the old classroom.

All, or nearly all, Slope County townships had a polling place until 1964. By then, county officials found they could no longer find enough adults to serve as election officials, and the County Commission consolidated the sites to nine. The Moord precinct was terminated around the end of the 20th Century, a victim of shrinking Slope County voting population. By 2004, there were six polling places; at the time of this writing, just three in the county.

The Rainy Buttes

The Rainies are three humps on the landscape to the south and west of our former farmstead. Baldy Butte, which we called Old Baldy, the smallest of the three, had a somewhat rounded top with crumbling ridges of chalky white and gray sandstone near the rim, giving it a likeness to a balding head; thus, its name. It stands between the much larger, flat-topped buttes, East Rainy and West Rainy and was located nearest our farmstead, which was three-quarters of a mile, or 10 minutes' walk, from Baldy's base.

Winter blizzards in our township often left snow drifts several feet deep, blocking roads, making farm chores difficult, and even killing livestock. After such a storm, the cliffs and draws on the south side of Old Baldy, which is the downwind side in a snow storm, are buried in snow. That was an open invitation to kids to grab sleds and sliders and head for Baldy. Lacking a fancy store-bought toboggan, we found an alternative in a 1950 Dodge car's engine hood. It had a strip of chrome down its center, which served as a keel to help our toboggan stay its course. We attached a lead rope, and the hood became our snow craft for three or four of us to pile on and fly down a favorite draw in Old Baldy where snow had covered *at least most* of the big boulders. The front rider was assigned to announce the right moment for bailing out. However, with our craft kicking up a flurry of snow, the scout wasn't always able to see the barbed wire fence coming up fast at the bottom of the slope. Thus, we sustained some bumps and bruises, and some winter jackets and mittens did get torn, but riding the Dodge hood left many fun memories.

Old Baldy was, in fact, a part of my life year round. When driving home from New England, it hung over the Flying M in my windshield view. Dad rented the butte from Tom Sather, our nearest neighbor who also lived just below the base of the butte. We used it as pasture for our milk cows and brood cows, especially when rainfall was plentiful enough to green up the native grasses. We were fortunate to have Beauty hanging around the farmstead when we had cattle on Old Baldy. It shortened the trip considerably if one could grab her bridle and ride her bareback up to the butte to get the milk cows turned in the direction of evening milking. Even without the horse, it was usually a pleasant task to walk to get the milk cows, and Buck, or whichever dog we had at the time, would run ahead and get the milk cows pointed toward home.

Chokecherries

The stands of chokecherry trees in the Rainy Buttes' draws provided a tangy treat when the berries ripened in

August. But they make the mouth pucker, so if you were already thirsty and weren't carrying any water, the berries afforded little relief. We also had a competitive, though disruptive, game to entertain visiting friends or cousins. The butte's top is littered with sandstone rocks of every size and shape, and we would find disk-shaped ones or roundish boulders that we freed to hurdle down the butte and into the fields below. Never mind that farmers who owned the fields below had already suffered the drudgery of clearing rocks from the same tracts. They didn't appreciate repairing fences that our stampeding rocks wound find. I recall having to do fence repairs many times around the butte to ensure our cows stayed in the pasture, but also a couple of times to repair our rock-rolling damage.

East Rainy and West Rainy both have somewhat flat crowns and are much bigger than Old Baldy. West Rainy Butte is about 1.5 miles west of our former farmstead; East Rainy, about the same distance south of the farmstead. East Rainy, with its long cliff of gray and white rock along its rim, plus a spring that ran from the rocks below that cliff year round, was our favorite for hiking, especially with visiting friends. Hiking to the rolling prairie that capped the butte's broad flat top was a workout by itself, and the scene from there was spectacular. The sky there suffers no pollution and isn't cloudy most of the time, so towns within about 20 miles of the butte are often clearly visible. We'd climb around in the crevasses and small caves in the long cliff, and look for unusual rocks and artifacts.

The East Rainy's cap rock (the butte's rock rim is the outer edge of the cap rock) has been sitting there for about 28 million years. A gold mine of discovery awaits paleontologists who will dig there some day. The tops of the Rainy Buttes, nearby Chalky Buttes, some other pieces of rugged landscape to the west and south are in a geologic strata called White River, which is rich in relics of North America's early mammals. Twenty-eight million years ago, an early version of the horse, called mesohippus, thrived on the continent. It grew only two feet tall and had three-toed feet instead of hooves. The region also had hordes of another grazing animal, called <u>oreodonts</u>, related to modern swine and camels. One of them, the Merycoidodon, was especially populous during some of the same periods.

Bob Gardner, my lifelong friend who has studied Northern Plains Indian history and our area's paleontology, mentored me a little with these pages. He said the top of the Rainy Buttes are actually the bottom of an ancient river that set down layers of sandstone. Then water from the melting of the last big glacier eroded the region round the buttes, leaving only the buttes sticking up from the landscape.

Our own pursuit of artifacts on the buttes were focused much more on recent relics of human history, such as stone tools and arrowheads from American Indians. Burial sites can be identified because the soil's layers and makeup are altered when a grave is dug and filled, so the stand of grass differs from surrounding grass, even though the species of grasses may be much the same as in the surrounding topsoil.

Bob has a bevy of Rainy Buttes historical anecdotes and footnotes. Early cattle drives, herding cattle up from the Southern Plains to the first western Dakota ranches passed by and between the buttes. Stone arrowheads picked up there can be up to 10,000 years old. He tells how the father of Sitting Bull, the famous Hunkpapa Lakota (Sioux) chief, was killed in a Crow Indians attack around East Rainy.

We were given a wonderful inducement for East Rainy hiking trips in the form of a set of U.S. Army infantry gear that Leon toted home in 1955, when he finished his two years with the U.S. Army. It included a heavy canvas pup tent and backpack, a canteen, ammo belt and mess kit. Rick recalls that, on a Sunday morning at Grandma Maixner's house after his Army discharge, Leon said that he had a pup tent for us upstairs and Rick says he ran immediately to look. He said it was never clear to him whether Leon intended his whole stash of gear as a gift, or couldn't bear to tell his little cousins otherwise after he saw how impressed we were with the booty.

There were two versions of gathering rocks on the Flying M. One was rock picking, for which you wear gloves to collect big ugly rocks that lie in fields or hide in the soil and break your field tilling machinery when it hits them. You stack them onto a trailer if you are in the field to pick rocks. Or, if your tilling machinery finds one in the ground that you want to remove from the field, you lift it to a convenient toting place on your tractor or tiller. During my years on the farm, we built a respectable pile of rocks – mostly sandstone – in the pasture over the hill from the farmhouse. The pile served as a backstop for our bullets when we wanted to target practice.

Knife River flint point

Occasionally, we'd run into an attractive section of petrified tree trunk in a field, and we would keep it as a landscape piece around the house. In general, field rock picking was, fortunately, a low priority task to do when the harvest of grain and hay was done or after a rain when fields were too muddy for other farming operations.

The other type of rock picking was to hunt for rare rocks and other fossils: archeological, paleontological and rock johnnie fun. The Rainy Buttes' flat tops, about 3,300 feet above sea level, stood perched about 250 feet above the surrounding landscape, thus served as a great landmark and lookout location for native people for thousands of years before Europeans arrived. Further, two types of dense siliceous rock, called Rainy Buttes Chert and Knife River Flint were

Rainy Buttes chert

created millions of years ago in our region and were used by Indians for thousands of years to fashion tools and weapons. The orange and multi-colored chert is indigenous to the Rainy Buttes area fields and hillsides. Meanwhile, clumps of the flint were mined for more than 10,000 years from a quarry about 80 miles north of the buttes. It was highly prized across North America because, like the chert, it breaks and sheers in predictable ways so that sharp-edged scrapers, knives, arrowheads and so forth can be readily formed. Thus, the flint was widely used and traded across the continent, and both intact and broken pieces of the flint and chert are found throughout the buttes and hilltops of the Flying M area.

This mallet, which I found on a hillside, was a vital tool to someone centuries ago.

I went "arrowhead hunting" sometimes, just a half century after farming started in Rainy Butte Township. Since the Flying M was at a crossroads for thousands of years of Indian travel, hunting, and tool- and weapon-making, remnants of paleo Indian tools and weapons could often be spotted, especially on the tops of hills and knolls, where erosion had eroded topsoil and exposed rocks, and in fields where plows had flipped rocks to the surface. Occasionally, a prize such as the big rock hammer (see photo) that I found in a field hillside near the farmstead would show itself in a field being disked or plowed.

I'll report here on a wild and unusual event that occurred beside and above the West Rainy Butte. The incident was a blazing UFO visit, witnessed by my Mom and four siblings in an early spring evening of 1967. That year was a busy one in our part of the Northern Plains for seeing extraterrestrial phenomenon. The National Investigations Committee on Aerial Phenomena, a UFO research group, calls 1967 the "Mother of all Sighting Waves" in North America. Several people across the Dakotas and Montana, including U.S. Air Force pilots and Minuteman Missile crews, reported sightings similar to what my family observed. For myself, I was home summers at the time but away at college in other seasons, so I missed the show they saw and can only report my siblings' and Mom's accounts. They had all piled into a car that raced toward the UFO perched above the West Rainy.

Fran recalls that Frank Reisenauer, whose farmstead was about a half mile northeast of ours, called to ask about a brilliant light hovering over the West Rainy. From our house, she could see something appearing "like a huge mercury vapor light" over the south end (from her vantage point) of the butte, which begins a little more than a mile west of our house. Joe drove our station wagon, with Mom in the front seat and Fran, Laura Lu and Darcy in the back seat, heading north to our mailbox, then west on the township road to get a closer look at the object. The troupe lost sight of the object for a bit, probably because the south end of the butte obstructed their view as the car traveled west. Says Fran: "When Joe turned on the car lights, it raised up quickly so we could see it, then in like a snap of the fingers, it sped away so fast that it was just a dot on the horizon."

Darcy, then 10 or 11 years of age, the youngest observer, gives a very similar account. "Laura Lu was crying; she didn't want to come. I told her, then stay here by yourself. So she came, scared as hell and crouched down on the floor in the back seat. We took off [in the car] and thought we'd keep the lights off and maybe sneak up on it. The UFO was hovering above the left hand [south] side of the butte, and I believe it was sitting between us and the butte. We could tell what size it was. I could see the size in perspective with the butte, and it was, you know, like 400 or 500 feet across. At least that big. It looked like two saucers put together – the standard shape they say UFOs are. And I remember the red blinking light underneath it. When we tried to drive closer, it went straight up into the air. It didn't make any noise. Then in just a blink of your eyes, all you could see is, way on the horizon, a little red dot." She also notes that neighbors who lived on farmsteads near the butte, but on its north side, did not report seeing the object but did report brief electrical power outages the same evening.

One funny twist to this story is that Joe, always the jokester, had considered UFO sightings reported in the area to be malarkey. He had set up a bogus UFO event from our farmstead within weeks before the real thing showed up over the West Rainy. Dad had a high intensity, 110-volt spotlight. Joe shined it alternately through red and blue glass objects, creating a little show in the sky. He trolled Bob Rotering, an area farmer, and his wife to the farmstead that night with his light show. Perhaps a take-home from this UFO story is that the tranquil Flying M could be a happening place at times.

Our Field and Garden Crops

Cutting seed potatoes, planting, harvesting, storing and processing the spuds for our table, plus selling sacks of them, was all part of life on the Flying M.

When selecting crops to grow, farmers want to choose plants that will flourish with the local temperatures, rainfall and length of growing season and produce bountifully. In southwest North Dakota, our farm saw long, very cold winters and usually chilly and wet springs. Summers were short and mostly hot and dry, with showers and thunderstorms that came on quickly, raced through, and left the sky blue and the sun shining within an hour. So we grew wheat, sold into the market for making flour, plus barley and oats, mostly to feed our own farm animals. We had field corn, which grows into tall, bulky plants that we chopped for silage. (Silage is whole corn plants that are chopped up and pickled in their own juice and fed to cattle. It is kind of like making sauerkraut with corn.) Plus we had a small tract of sweet corn near the farmyard. It was an extension of our vegetable garden and provided corn on the cob for our table for a few weeks in August and often early September. We also sliced corn off the cob and Mom canned it in jars. But we had a large chest freezer and I think the kernels were mostly bagged and frozen. We grew alfalfa, clover and grasses in creek bank areas and other lowlands that offered lots of moisture for hay crops to flourish. But we grew similar hay crops on hilly tracts, where such plants are critical to protect the topsoil from erosion.

Spuds were another crop that often put a few dollars in the Maixner siblings' pockets. We seeded potatoes in an acre or so of fertile, low-lying land a short walk from our house. In late spring, Dad would plow open furrows a few inches deep, and my siblings and I would drop the seedlings (slices of sprouting potatoes) of Pontiacs, a red baking-style potato, into the furrows. Then he'd come back with the plow to throw the soil back in the opposite direction to cover the seed. One spring, perhaps Dad was short on kids available to seed potatoes, and necessity served as midwife to invention. He found a section of stove pipe, probably from the pipe that had served the coal stove in our old house, and wedged it into the frame of the plow so that the bottom end was positioned strategically over where the trailing plowshare would cut its furrow. Then, as Bill took over on the tractor and drove very slowly down the field, Dad sat on the plow with a big pail of potato pieces, dribbling them down the pipe and into planting position.

Anyway, we would weed the spuds and harvest them in early fall in a similar procedure with the plow. The plowshares were set just deep enough to turn the spuds to the top of the soil while hitting very few with the plow. We would gather them into buckets, then fill big burlap bags and sell some of them to neighbors, for example, and bring some to extended family. The rest were dumped into a bin in our root cellar for our own winter supply.

On many farms, a root cellar is separated from the house and often dug into the side of a hill that has a steep slope so all but the doorway to the cellar is underground. When my parents planned their new house, they took advantage of the opportunity to include a root cellar as part of the house. They extended the basement under the garage at one end and put the cellar under it, then separated it from the rest of the house with a cement block wall and a thick plywood door to minimize transfer of heat into the root cellar. That way, it didn't freeze because it was below ground level ground yet remained cool for winter storage of root and tuber crops, which is why it is called a root cellar, and for jars of canned vegetables, pickled meats, and wine.

Also, the house was built during the first "Red Scare," when there was fear of nuclear bombs in an attack by the Russian-controlled Soviet Union. So people were encouraged to have a "bomb shelter," and our root cellar, with its foot-thick concrete ceiling, would have served that purpose in protecting us from bombs hitting near the farmstead, but, of course, would not have saved us from high levels of radioactivity.

We raised cabbages that were shredded to make jars of sauerkraut, which were stored on shelves in the root cellar. Also often kept there were gallon jugs of Grandma Luella's chokecherry, rhubarb and other wines. Since the brothers' basement dorm was just a few steps from the cellar door, wine was sometimes illegally sipped by minors. Wine remaining in the jugs could be diluted with water to mask the crime.

Sweet corn and potatoes were grown on larger lowland tracts near the farmstead, and the rest of veggie production was on a level plot behind the house that was within easy reach with a hose from our water well there. Dad worked the topsoil with a field cultivator a couple of times to give us a loose, level soil surface, and we planted standard American fare: beets, carrots, cabbage, cucumbers, leaf lettuce, onions, radishes, string beans, squash, sweet peas and other greens at times. Mom directed and helped with planting, but the seeding, weeding and harvesting was kids' work for the younger siblings and whomever else was available. Our vegetable garden was not overly ambitious yet provided us with an assortment of products in summer and fall.

In fact, I recall that our kitchen canning operations, which Mom planned and directed, were more productive than the garden output. Not depending solely on our garden's bounty, she would get a deal on a dozen or more heads of cabbage, and we used a cabbage shredder – a broad wooden board with knives embedded in it – to produce dozens of quart and two-quart jars of sauerkraut. Bargains on crates of peaches or pears would mean dozens of jars of canned and frozen fruit. A special on cucumbers, or a big crop in Grandma Maixner's patch, promised lots of pickles.

Grandma Maixner's garden was more advanced than ours. She was the top gardener and veggie agronomist in our clan. It is hard to say for certain, but I might have spent as much time helping in her garden as our home patch. Her big garden, apple trees and berry patches were the envy of her neighbors. She devoted half of her two-stall garage to mushrooms, and she had thriving patches of raspberries and strawberries.

Flying M Critters

Growing up on a farm or ranch means learning about animals and having a range of relationships with them. Some are your pals and you protect them, and some, in turn protect you. Some are managed to produce milk and eggs. You don't want to hurt animals, yet some must be killed to produce meat.

On the farm, animals fall into three categories: pets, farm livestock and wildlife. The first two are on the farm; the latter, mostly outside the farmstead but not always. That means even the kids on farms that produce only crops but no livestock still learn about animals because of pets and wildlife. For me, animals were a part of my daily work, play, education, joy and sorrows.

Pets are, most often, dearest to the heart. For kids both in cities and on farms, pets are friends first of all. They are like family members, and they remain on the farm until they die naturally. That isn't the case for most livestock. What's more, pets on farms often have jobs. For both farms and city households, for example, cats control the population of rodents, and dogs often protect their masters and household.

But pets on farms generally have more jobs than city pets do. Beauty, our quarter horse mare, was first a pet for riding. In fact, she was Dad's Christmas gift to the family when I was about seven years old. Tom Sather's barn was just a short walk over the hill from our farmstead. Tom was elderly and had quit keeping livestock, so Dad asked him if he could hide Beauty for a couple of weeks in his vacant barn and feed her there until Christmas. Adding a horse to the family on Christmas morning was a huge surprise – I don't recall if she came with a ribbon or not.

Buck and I; East Rainy is on the horizon.

A saddle that Dad had for an earlier horse, named Snort, got only occasional use on Beauty and mostly by my older brothers. I would just grab her bridle, place its bit into her mouth, pull the straps over her head and climb aboard. She was a mature mare when we got her and already so people-friendly that when Joe or other younger siblings fell asleep on her riding bareback and slid to the ground she was likely to stand and wait for us to climb back on.

Beauty had tricks. She would lift her front right hoof if you said, "shake." She was skilled at releasing several types of pasture gate handles and catches, which were typically wire hoops that dropped over the top of the gate post or levers that were looped with chain around the top of the gatepost. Usually, the worst consequence of Beauty's mischief was that our cattle were released to wherever they wanted to wander. Most often, fortunately, they just headed straight for the greenest, leafiest plants on their horizon and began munching. So roundup was not terribly difficult.

But on a few cases of her gate-opening mischief, Beauty found the door left open at the feed storage house that held milled barley or oats for cattle in the feedlot. A horse with access to ground grain will usually grossly overeat, and the grain then swells up in their stomach, and that can kill them. She also once found her way through the milk separator room and to the feed bin for the milk cows. We found Beauty in grain binging situations a few times. Rick recalled that Dad filled a bottle with mineral oil and somehow forced the oil down her throat, making her clear her bowels and probably saving her life. Besides the mineral oil dousing, we had to walk her for hours to encourage her digestive system to keep processing and moving the grain through her.

Dad had Beauty bred when I was very young, yet I do remember when she delivered a colt, named Coke. Sadly, Coke was injured within a few months of birth when he tried to catch up to his mother after one of us took off on Beauty. He ended up tangled in a barbed wire fence east of the yard. The barbs tore into his shoulder. Dad gave him to Leo Dubizar, the New England blacksmith, who sewed up the tear and kept Coke. I guess he figured Leo had more time for nursing a colt than he did.

Beauty lived for perhaps a dozen years after that. Oddly, she disliked coming close to the house even though she was so comfortable with people. But on the day she died, she walked to the house and up to the side door, located in the garage, and nudged or bumped the door. Mom went to the door and found the mare waiting there. She had to drive here out of the garage, then closed the overhead door. Within hours, she was found dead nearby. Dad and Mom understood she had tried to come home to die.

Buck arrived when I was a preschooler. He was an English Shepherd, a breed in the collie family, and was the first dog I recall on the farmstead. He was typical for his breed: an intelligent, all-around farm dog who was excellent at herding cattle, watching and guarding the farmstead, plus playing with and protecting the family. Mom didn't dare to chase after us or to try to spank one of us kids in Buck's presence; he would threaten her, barking, growling and snarling. He was especially loyal to another task he assumed with no particular encouragement from the family. When we were all away for a few hours or days, he would hear our car approaching and would chase all cats loitering near the house to the dairy barn or otherwise away from where the cars were parked, and then come to greet us. He just didn't want to share homecoming strokes with cats.

After Buck's death of old age, our next dog, Duke, a black Labrador-retriever cross, helped us learn how different two very smart dogs can be. Duke was a gift from our Uncle Bob Steckman, a city guy and avid upland bird hunter. He quickly learned people-pleasing commands – speaking, rolling over, etc. – that Buck hadn't much taken to. For a pup, Duke followed directions quite well. But he didn't have a clue about what to do with cattle and would chase them in the wrong direction more often than not. Instead, he was a bird dog with a highly sensitive nose. He would catch the scent of the trail of a pheasant, partridge, mourning dove, or other bird, put his nose to the ground and follow the trail to its end, bird dinner or no. Then we would spend hours trying to find him within two-miles or so of the farmstead. Finally, one day Duke caught the scent of a bird or other critter and headed over the hill with his nose to the ground, and we saw no more of him.

After that, Flying M dogs were collies or collie crosses. We had a smart collie cross, named Patches, who was very adept at herding cattle. We produced a lot of meat scraps at our house, and we had a rule about not allowing our dog to get bones from cooked meat bones, which are brittle and can become like knives in the stomach. But she got into some leftover chicken bones, which punctured her stomach walls. Dad took her to the vet, but the bone shards had done their damage, and she was dead within a few days.

We had another collie cross also named Patches that was truly stupid and lacked the kind of brain needed for farm operations. She attacked the chickens, chased cattle in every direction, and so forth. I was in college then. Joe was the oldest sibling at home and got the assignment to shoot the dog and bury her behind the trees. He swore that if such an assignment came up again, someone else had to do it.

Then Dad got Cookie, a large collie, who was a great cattle dog, socially smart and good companion to Dad through the years when my younger siblings were finishing high school and heading off into adulthood. When asked to "whisper," she would make little murmuring sounds. Joe taught her, on the command, "get the cows, Cookie," to streak into the pasture to collect the milk cows. He would also tell her, "you stink, Cookie; take a bath," and she would jump into the big cattle drinking tank.

Heidi was a Saint Bernard-collie cross who Rick picked up from the farm of a family friend, Arnold Rotering, several years after I left the farm. She was to be a farm dog, so she lived at the central farmstead rather than at Rick's family house. Fortunately, she developed Cookie's best traits but was a lot bigger and loved bossing cattle. She once intercepted a bull headed straight at Rick, grabbing its nose with her teeth, swinging its head and putting a stop to the bull long enough for Rick to clear out. One of her tricks was smiling: If you asked her to smile she would bare her front teeth at you in a kind silly Snoopy smile.

Our dogs and horses were shared pets, but the Flying M always had an abundance of cats when I was growing up. So we could adopt a kitten as our own if we wished. I selected a long-haired gray one with white chest and feet.

I named him Shivers because he shivered when I picked him up. Also distinguishing was a slightly bobbed tail. It was clipped when he was still a kitten and he came up to the bike I was riding. The chain and sprocket caught his tail as I went to pedal away, crushing the tip of the tail before I could figure out how to release a screaming, howling kitten from sprocket and chain. A couple of weeks later, the injured tip dropped off.

With his bobbed tail, Shivers was a rangy looking, gritty fellow with wiry gray hair and white feet and markings. He earned and held alpha male status on the Flying M for several years, providing me a front row seat to observing social structure of domestic cats. Blacky, a tom perhaps two years younger, grew a little larger than Shivers and started challenging him. His insubordination was rewarded with lodging in the loft in the cow milking barn, the building that also provided a cat barracks near where skim milk was served in big pans. He had to sneak down from the loft to drink his milk after Shivers had left. But, not surprisingly, the day arrived when Shivers was holding out in the loft instead of Blacky. His reign had passed, and he didn't live a whole lot longer.

Our milk separator looked like this one. (Photo from Michelle Knows Antiques)

Blacky and Shivers had a little trick that was not especially fun for whomever milked the cows. When I had finished milking and was heading for the next room, the felines all knew what time of day it was. The easiest and quickest way for the tom in the loft to get to the milk bowl was to walk to the end of the top of the wooden stanchions that held the milk cows in their milking positions, then jump to my shoulders as I passed by. Especially in the summer, when I wore either a T-shirt or no shirt, a big tomcat anchoring himself on your shoulder was unnerving and sometimes painful.

With the two-gallon pasteurizer to fill, we used a good portion of daily milk production for drinking and cooking. All of the rest was poured into a separator which is a centrifuge machine. Our model was made by McCormick-Deering. Its stainless steel milk-handling parts were mounted on a dark red cast iron pedestal that had a long steel hand crank allowing the user to crank a flywheel at the rear of the machine up to a whining RPM. Maintaining the high centrifuge speed was necessary to separate the milk into cream and skim milk. The crank handle had a metal ball in its hollow core, and when it stopped dropping with a click each half turn of the crank, you knew the crank and the drum were moving fast enough to effectively separate the cream.

We kept the cream for our kitchen use or for sale to the New England creamery. Skim milk also had several uses: We poured some of it into buckets that had rubber teats at the base, stirred in some powdered supplement designed especially for weaned calves, and fed the mixture to young calves whose mothers we were milking. We poured some into the big pan on the separator room floor for cats to lap up. Sometimes we used it to make cottage cheese. And if the weaned calves were already several months old and did not need it any longer, we could just dump the excess.

Besides the cats' skim-milk feast in the separator room, they often gathered near the cows being milked, where they would wait for one of us to squirt a stream of warm milk directly from the cow's udder to their mouths. They swallowed eagerly at top speed, and then licked up spillage from their fur, relishing it as a tasty mess on fur that had to be groomed anyway.

The word "livestock" refers to animals that produce food on a farm. On our place, that started with cows for milking and hens for laying eggs. It included animals to be butchered for meat: cattle, pigs, chickens, turkeys and, for a short period, rabbits. We had a lot of cattle, and most of them were fattened to be sold to feedlot operators who would continue to fatten them for several months more before slaughter at meatpacking sites. Also, we hunted wildlife for meat, which I address later in my wildlife chapter.

Our chickens were in both the eggs and meat categories: Some hens were kept to mature and provide eggs, but then butchered after perhaps three years and used for soup meat. We didn't, however, butcher dairy cows when they got old. While we became accustomed to the bloody task of butchering some animals for meat, those that became like pets were sent elsewhere. When one milks the same cow for several years, she becomes sort of a pal. Plus much of the meat from an old dairy cow is of lesser quality. So our dairy cows went to market at retirement age.

Our beef-breed cattle were Hereford, Angus and crosses of the two breeds, plus often a few other cross-breeds of calves purchased for our feedlot. Fattening calves in our feedlot was a huge part of the farm's operations, so nearly all of them were sold into the cattle market to make beef. The calves from our cows were brought into the feedlot in October, and Dad bought more calves from other area farmers to make full use of the feedlot. They were fed corn silage, milled barley, hay and supplements until they were sold the next spring or early summer. Molasses was often blended with the milled grain, for example. It is a high-energy supplement that would help them thrive in our cold winters, and it enhanced their growth as well.

From my pre-teen years through high school, upon returning from school most days, I was helping to load our 1936 GMC truck with silage and grain and shoveling the feed mix into the long feed bunk along the edge of the feedlot, where the calves waited eagerly. It was a two-person job, or a longer task for one because then one had to stop shoveling and climb behind the steering wheel to move the truck ahead before continuing to shovel.

We butchered a few fattened calves and hogs on the farm for our own food. Quarters and halves of carcasses were often sold to extended family or friends, or traded with them, for example, in return for other use of equipment or their labor.

When kids spend time with meat animals and become close to them, killing them becomes troubling. However, where the beef cattle were concerned, the Slope County Fair provided one convenient outlet market for selling meat animals that had become pets. Maixner kids belonged to the Rainy Buttes 4-H Club. 4-H is sort of the farming version of Girl Scouts and Boy Scouts of America wrapped into one. For us, it meant monthly meetings with lessons on citizenship, leadership, raising crops and livestock, safety with power equipment, and so forth, along with an afternoon to visit other farm kids from our area.

We were not especially avid 4-Hers, but at some point we were allowed to select a steer or heifer from Dad's herd as a 4-H project, keeping it around the farmstead to teach it to lead with a halter (called halter-breaking), feeding it plenty so it was as muscled and plump as possible, then grooming it to look its best for an appearance at the fair. Show calves were auctioned off at the end of the fair, providing both meat for someone else's table and college savings for the Maixner kids who showed them. Plus it meant we didn't send pet 4-H calves directly to slaughter or have to eat a pet calf at our own table. It was possible, perhaps likely, that meat from 4-H calves, months after they were sold at the fair and went to slaughter, did, unbeknown to us, end up at a table where we were eating.

The 4-H calf experiences varied from one sibling to the next. I believe I often helped brothers and sisters with theirs, but did not bring more than one to the fair myself, since I had other summer jobs, such as farm work for my uncles, to build cash for college. After my senior year, I measured farmers' cropland for the U.S. Department of Agriculture to certify their acreages in compliance with USDA crop subsidy programs. However, sister Fran had three or more calves, she recalls. Thus, at up to $300 for a 1,000-pound calf, they added a lot to her college purse.

One exception to our farm's no-pets-for-dinner policy was Fran's lamb, Baa. As a pre-teen, she took to bottle-feeding a baby lamb that a ewe a friend's ranch in South Dakota. Healthy ewes, especially in the white-faced breeds, often bear twins. But if they decide they have enough milk for just one, they reject the other, resulting in an orphan, which is called a bum lamb. Without intervention, they starve. Fran bottle-fed Baa, and it was allowed to run loose in the farmyard. So it got plenty to eat. I may have been one of the lynching party who converted the fattened lamb into chops and roasts. Fran recalls that she tasted roast or chop from Baa Baa, but one taste was more than enough for her. Brother Joe recalls that he adopted at least one bum lamb from Ralph Urlacher's nearby ranch, and it was harvested for meat as well.

By the time I was returning home in summers to farm with Dad and my uncles, I had absorbed a lot of experiences with farm animals. As was then the case on most Slope County farms, our cows were bred to give birth to calves in April: Late enough so winter weather stresses are avoided but early enough so the calves mature somewhat before they are weaned in the fall. That means all the cows were having babies within the same few weeks and, even with our modest herd, the Flying M became a bustling bovine nursery. Dad tried to keep an eye on expectant mothers, especially the heifers, the females having their first baby. They usually needed no help; just their own space and nobody to bother them. Still, especially for the heifers, we sometimes took watch when Dad couldn't be there and a cow was showing physical signs that she was ready to deliver a calf.

Calves usually leave their mothers head first from the birth canal, just as with human babies. However, calves have four long, skinny legs that need to be born, too, and must be pointed in the right direction. Most often, the front feet come from the mother first, tucked against the head, then the rest of the calf. It is usually okay, too, if the hind feet come first. But once is a while, the calf is turned butt-first (called "breach"). When that happened it was time to summon Dad, because the calf would die in the cow if someone did not reach into the cow and pull feet out first. That birth canal emergency job is not for a youngster but is something I helped with occasionally after my high school years, and was another of the valuable nature lessons on a diversified farm.

We learned about poultry, too. Mom ordered 500 baby chicks each spring for arrival via the U.S. mail. I helped release them from their cardboard cartons in a coop, or chicken house, that featured a "brooder," a sort of heated umbrella under which the chicks would gather as though under momma's wing to stay warm. I enjoyed watching them grow quickly through months of feeding and watering them.

Chickens need protection. In the daytime, our laying hens roamed around the farmyard, picking up stray grain and seeds, but also bits of rock to grind the food in their gizzards. The frequent moving of grain and animal feed and hay around our farmstead area left a lot of chow for the hens. Plus a range of grass and weeds flourished in some areas and offered nutrition. And in the winter we dumped kitchen scraps in their fenced area to supplement their grain rations. Hens will find their own way to a roost provided in their coop, and we closed the entry door at night so a badger, fox or stray dogs couldn't attack them.

Our big flock of young chickens, meanwhile, spent their days inside a small yard enclosed by a 10-foot-high net-wire fence to protect them. Confined young chickens, left to their own devices, will often single out one or more unfortunates to pick on and will peck them to death. To discourage that, we set out blocks of milk whey for them to peck instead. Perhaps because of whey's high protein content, it deterred much of the pecking. We did, however, have to apply a gob of terrible tasting goop (to chickens) to the back of the head of any bird who had been selected for abuse, and it did deliver a real disincentive. A chicken pecked the goop just once and quickly became very busy scraping its beak on the ground, trying to wipe the stuff off.

Come mid-summer, I helped butcher young chickens as they reached "fryer" size, about four to five pounds live weight. It meant chopping off heads, dunking the birds quickly into boiling water to loosen the feathers, stripping off the feathers, opening the body cavity and removing internal organs, boxing the carcasses for delivery to local customers, or cutting up the birds and wrapping the pieces for our winter food supply.

Farm kids tend to inherit an attitude about livestock animals that is foreign to many urban kids, who are naturally conflicted with combining the role of protecting, feeding and nurturing animals with the act of slaughtering them for their food supply. Farm kids accept both roles, and I think one result is an especially strong aversion to giving any animal unnecessary pain. While I could chop off a chicken's head, or slaughter a pig or steer, I was troubled when New England boy scouts, for example, laughed when telling about putting firecrackers in a frog's mouth and lighting the fuse during an outing. Fortunately, the dad of one of those friends caught the comments and reprimanded them, saying it was a cruel thing to do. It wasn't funny to me at all, and I remember the little incident to this day.

Wildlife

On a cool, foggy morning in the spring of 1958, we were planting wheat, and I was sipping coffee with Dad in the truck cab at the end of a field. He pointed to two white birds with huge, black-tipped wing spans lifting off from Tom Sather's creek area and said: "Take a good look. Those are whooping cranes, and you won't see them here very often."

Herds of 50 or more pronghorn antelope often gathered in our fields and pastures.

While growing up, we saw an array of ring-neck pheasants, Hungarian partridge, Mallard and other ducks, red-tailed hawks, meadowlarks and other birds. Whoopers are an endangered bird that migrates through that part of North Dakota. I don't think that I did see more of them on our farm, although I have seen them a few times since in other locations. Nonetheless, the menagerie of wild animals in Rainy Butte Township left me many memories of observing their beauty, skills and habits, but also of hunting wildlife to harvest meat or furs and skins.

Rabbits were wildlife and, for a brief period, livestock as well on the Flying M. We covered the floor of a corner storage room in the milking barn with straw and raised some tame rabbits there. They could also become wildlife because, unlike tame farm livestock, if they escaped we would not likely see them again. The rabbits' room had a single window for daylight, and I expect their confinement prompted the reoccurring bouts they had with respiratory and other diseases that killed many of them. We frequently treated their water with Terramycin, an antibiotic, to arrest outbreaks. We did butcher and roast a few, but it turned out that tending to a dozen or fewer rabbits was more chore than it was worth. Besides, rabbits are very cute and killing them was not fun. The little enterprise was short-lived: just a year or two, I think.

Cats, like rabbits, reproduce rapidly if not neutered. Because we butchered some rabbits and lost others to disease, the brief rabbit population was never big on our farm. We needed cats, meanwhile, for rodent control and we always had plenty of them, since we wouldn't know what to do with tiny cat organs to neuter them, and paying veterinarians to do that job wasn't affordable. So our cats reproduced as nature allowed. They were usually a healthy bunch and, with typically two or three adult females on the place, each spring and summer seasons would bring perhaps 10 to 20 kittens.

The older siblings on the farm had a job of dispatching the surplus of cats. Favorites especially prized by family members were most often spared, but Dad would ask one of us to thin the herd, or sometimes, I think, we decided by consensus what should be done to keep the feline population at bay. Then, some were killed with a .22 Caliber rifle at the farm's landfill, for example, or bagged in a gunnysack and drowned in a creek nearby. We all liked cats, so the intent was to make deaths as quick and painless as possible. I recall one summer when I was 13 or 14, I think, when I returned from dispatching the kitty oversupply in our stock dam. My sisters met me on the return and reproached me angrily for murdering kitties. I felt bad about it. For me, the drownings had been a very unpleasant job that I had taken my turn to do.

Hunting was a guys' thing on our farm. Leon loved hunting and accumulated a collection of antique classics as well as modern precision rifles. For the rest of us, we hunted regularly but it was usually of more casual interest. We had just a basic assortment of rifles and shotguns in our front hallway closet for family use. In the autumn, I might opt for the .410 or 20-guage shotgun to hunt upland birds. I enjoyed taking a .22 caliber rifle to walk for an hour or two on a winter weekend afternoon to hunt jackrabbits or fox in the winter. The pelts of both spelled cash in the pocket, but I was as likely to bring home flint arrowheads or other interesting rocks as fur-bearing trophies.

For many years, my Uncle Bob Steckman would drive from Omaha in October to hunt pheasants on our farm and in the rest of our township and other nearby areas. A few landowners in our area began posting signs prohibiting hunting on their land, but most nearby land was open for hunting or, alternatively, the owner would grant us permission. After driving more than 500 miles with his kids, he was fired up to hunt, and a few of us would hunt pheasants with him. Once, one of us asked: "Uncle Bob, if you saw a rooster pheasant perched on a "No Hunting" sign, what would you do?" With little pause, he said, "I'd shoot the pheasant and then the sign."

Jackrabbits were worth $1 to $1.50 apiece at the local fur trader in winter months when their fur was white, but not the rest of the year. So we often had a .22 caliber rifle in a car or truck in the winter to pick up some fur income. A favorite was hunting jackrabbits at night. They are nocturnal and were often near roads at night and would show up in our headlights. We also used a spotlight to beam on them, momentarily blinding them, which usually provided several seconds for a good shot while they were still sitting. But rabbits are a small target, and they were usually at least, say, 40 yards distant, so hitting them on the run was a very low-percentage shot. In high school and college years, it was always a treat to go night hunting for jackrabbits with a pal or two and, if available in my college years, a few beers. Our spotlight plugged into a cigarette lighter outlet, which meant we could use it in any of the vehicles. But rabbit hunting with Bob Gardner and his dad's utility pickup truck was great because the spotlight was mounted on top of the cab, with its steering control inside where it was warm and easy to reach.

We also hunted some wildlife as meat sources: white-tailed and mule deer, pronghorn antelope, ring-necked pheasants, Hungarian partridge, grouse, etc. The state specifies autumn hunting seasons for those species, and we would generally hunt them in that season, though not always within specified seasons if we were hunting on our own land. Game wardens did not frequent our township, and we figured that we provided the animals' habitat and could occasionally harvest a few of them. It was sort of like farming the wildlife. We never had to learn if a warden would agree with that theory.

Aside from sport hunting to provide meat or fur pelts, we shot some predator or nuisance animals either on or near the farmstead to protect our chickens and other livestock. Skunks, for example, were shot if seen near the farmstead because they have a penchant for eggs and can be infected with rabies. We had coyotes around, but I don't recall ever shooting one. They were shy of the farmyard, especially because we always had a farm dog.

For a couple of years, we farmed pheasants, so to speak, instead of hunting them. Owing to droughts and severe winter weather, the North Dakota pheasant population plunged in the early 1960s. In response, the N.D. Game and Fish Department asked willing farmers to take 50 pheasant chicks, raise them until they could fly and release them.

We accepted that task for two years. Most of our earlier house was used to as a chicken house and had a high fenced area at one end for the fowl. At the other end was a small entry room. So we cut a little entrance door for the pheasants at the back of that room and erected a high wire-netting cage outside, where the fledglings would first try their wings in flights of about eight to ten feet. We found a mom for them among our Leghorn laying hens. We elected a "cluck," our name for ones that were especially protective of their eggs. We fed and watered the chicks, and the cluck kept them under her wing. She also taught them what to eat among the grains and seeded plants we provided them, crucial education for their later survival.

When the birds reached two to three months of age, it was a thrill to take them to the top of the hill just behind their pheasant house and let them go. Despite never having had room to fly more than a few feet at once, they all simply took flight and soared about a half-mile to neighbor Tom Sather's creek and grove of trees.

A fringe benefit of herding cows or operating a tractor or other field implement was the front row seat such jobs afforded for observing wildlife. I still recall two bobolinks, which are six-inch-long songbirds, dive-bombing a red-tailed hawk, who said uncle and hightailed it out of the bobolinks' proclaimed territory. The hawk may have come too close to their chicks. I saw Bobolinks conduct such defense maneuvers quite often. And when cutting an alfalfa field for hay in early June, it was common to come upon a deer and her fawn bedded down in the greenery, or any of an array of birds and other mammals.

But field work brought sad moments, too, when the machinery maimed or killed animals despite one's efforts to steer clear of them. When cutting alfalfa or grass with a mower or swather, for example, the cutting bar on those machines could slice through any part of a small animal in its path. Most either ducked down against the ground, letting the cutting bar pass over, or ran or flew off ahead of the machine. Quite often I would have to stop the swather or mower, get down into the field with a hammer or other tool, and euthanize an animal that had lost its legs, or was otherwise maimed. That was a dreary task.

Yay for Electricity and Mechanical Innovation!

As noted earlier, our move from old house to new in late 1955 was much more than a truck ride to a new building on the same farmstead. For the people of Rainy Butte Township, the 1950s spelled the arrival of electrical power and accelerated improvements in machines, transportation, building materials and more. I recall that, after necessities such as beds, clothing and dishes, a lot of our past was left behind at the old house with its coal stove and outdoor toilet. The new house was larger, and I recall the place looking roomy but also a bit spare. Mom began picking up furnishings and appliances via the Montgomery Ward and Sears catalogs, the local Gardner & Zeren Hardware and Gambles stores, and elsewhere.

Dad had taken short courses in electrical wiring, welding and more on the GI bill after his World War II service as an Army Air Force mechanic. Leon was a wizard with mechanical and carpentry tools. They added to the farm's conveniences and facilities. Dad and Frank Heick, for example, built a long and sturdy kitchen table to handle a household ten strong.

Leon took an old gasoline engine (perhaps the one that had driven our abandoned wringer washer) and converted it into our first air compressor. He welded its exhaust shut, took the ceramic center out of a spark plug and brazed a metal tube into it in its place, then attached a hose so that air was pumped from the old motor's cylinder head.

That first, homemade compressor was powered by – ta-dah! – an electric motor. The first electrical lines were being built into much of rural America in the 1940s, and Slope Electric Cooperative, the rural co-op serving our area, extended service to our farm in about 1950, three or four years after my parents bought our farm. At the time, in our first house, we had a very limited, 110-volt service for lighting and little else. I believe we had just a few ceiling lights and lamps, and the refrigerator in the kitchen there burned kerosene, cooled by an evaporation/condensation process. We don't talk today about "making" a warm bath, but that is what we did then. We heated water in a reservoir at the back of the coal stove and big buckets of water on the stovetop. At bath time, we took turns in a big galvanized steel tub that was placed on the kitchen floor for Saturday evening's rub-a-dub.

Thus, the new house meant stepping up to full electrical power, with 110-volt outlets, plus a few 220-volt ones, which supplied energy to appliances such as stoves, clothes driers and, in the shop, the arc welder. Electric power was a tremendous advancement, with laundry being a prime example. Monday was clothes washing day and it meant Mom and available kids washing a week's dirty clothes from at least ten people, including diapers from the youngest. In the old house, Monday morning meant starting a gasoline engine to power the agitator for washing the clothes and running the wringer (which squeezed the washed garments between two rolling rubber cylinders, accomplishing basically what a current spin cycle does). Shortly before or after the move to the new house, that engine was replaced with an electric motor. Within a few years after the move, a robust wheat harvest or two and a strong market for fattened cattle allowed my parents to buy a conventional electric washer and dryer for our utility room. However, when several loads were being washed, we still hung perhaps most of our clothes to dry on a clothes line near the house.

In about 1957, Mom's youngest brother, Frank Steckman, brought us a black-and-white-screen Phillips television, our first set. It went into the living room. It was tuned on for early evening news broadcasts and a few other programs that we enjoyed: Texas Rangers, Zorro, Highway Patrol and Sea Hunt during the weekdays. On Saturday nights: Jackie Gleason, Lawrence Welk, Gunsmoke and Have Gun Will Travel (Paladin). Then it was turned off for the evening. The broadcast stations all signed off overnight in those years. The TV was moved to the basement when it was finished off a few years later with a family rec room and boys' bedrooms.

Mechanization had huge impacts, of course, on farming operations in the 1950s and 1960s. We saw the adoption of very helpful power tools and machinery that saved physical labor and vastly increased output: Our arc welder, for example, that allowed many machinery repairs right in the farm shop. Electrically powered pumps drew well water for household and livestock water needs.

However, a windmill in the middle of the yard continued to fill our main cattle watering tank, and was a handy second source of water if there was trouble with the well serving the house, or if we had an electric power outage. We had an aquifer less than 50 feet from the surface, but the water was in a layer of sand, which could fill in the cavity opened for pumping water and even plug up the pump located down in the aquifer. Later, we dug wells much deeper, into productive water tables, but the water was not as pleasant to the taste as that from the shallow wells, so my parents usually fetched water from the windmill pump for their coffee.

Shoveling grain is a slow, backbreaking job, and machinery gradually reduced much of the drudgery. In my earliest memories, most of the grain trucked in from the field had to be shoveled into a bin. Then, when it was sold, it was shoveled back into a truck and hauled to market, where the truck was driven up into the grain elevator's platform and shoveled out the back of the box and through a big opening in the floor. It was all a whale of a lot of shoveling.

For moving grain from a truck box to a high grain bin, our first important labor saver arrived when I was still a preschooler, I think, and it was called a blower. It worked like a huge vacuum cleaner. Grain was shoveled from a truck box into a hopper (shaped like a tub) at the base of a long, flexible metal pipe, where a big fan powered by a farm tractor's engine blew the grain up the pipe, directing it into a door or window near the top of the grain bin. While I was growing up, however, the blower and a lot of the shoveling were replaced by mobile grain elevators, which are long metal pipes that encased metal augers, mounted on frames with wheels. The augers are driven by gasoline engines mounted on the elevators. You could just roll them from job to job and, for example, lift grain to a truck box as it poured out of the bottom of a grain bin, or into a granary as it poured out of a truck box.

About the same time, hydraulic lifts were becoming popular features for truck boxes, letting a farmer just tip the front of his truck box up and let grain flow out its back door instead of having to shovel it out. In the mid-1950s, Dad bid successfully on a 1946 Chevy truck being sold off by the North Dakota Highway Department. It had a hydraulic lift box, so Dad replaced its rock-hauling box with a grain box and he was good to go.

Labor saving changes were also on the way for hay making, which had been at least as backbreaking as handling grain. Cut and dried grass, alfalfa, oats or other hay could be mechanically raked into windrows or bunches, but then had to be forked by hand onto hay wagons, then forked from the wagons to build a haystack. Many of the farmers, including Dad's brothers, Stan and Al, bought Farmall (International Harvester) tractors, equipped with hydraulically controlled hay forks to push hay windrows into piles, then lift them onto trucks or to the top of haystacks. Dad bought a comparable loader, brand-named DuAll, and mounted it onto a Minneapolis Moline Model U tractor. The DuAll included an alternative loading tool: A scoop for hauling dirt, manure and such, and it was used extensively on our place.

The Model U was also known by Flying M brothers as the Scenic Cruiser because its transmission gear ratios assigned a very high speed, as farm tractors go, for its "road gear," as we called it, and because boys tired of driving a tractor in the field at one to five miles per hour will go for maximum velocity when given the option. The U's fifth gear was much faster than the fourth gear, though it afforded very little power. So the only place it could be used was on an open road. No matter that years of using the DuAll attachments loosened the steering hardware's control of the front wheels and made steering the thing in a straight line pretty difficult. But we tended to open that baby up on the road, then stay focused on keeping the tractor between the ditches as we bounded along at about 20 miles per hour.

Before buying the DuAll, Dad would hire Bob Grant and others to help with haying. Bob was a distant cousin to Mom and was part American Indian. He was tall and had such arm and back strength that he broke sturdy hickory fork handles lifting enormous bunches of hay. So Dad asked him to grip the metal base of the handle with one hand, thus sparing the fork handle.

Near the end of my farming years, one very welcome mechanical upgrade was a self-propelled Model 35 Owatonna swather. Dad bought it in 1966 from my cousin LaVryl Wolff Feland's husband, Marshall, who ran a lumberyard and had secured an Owatonna franchise.

As it happened, Marshall drove his own truck to Owatonna, in southeast Minnesota, to pick up the machine. I rode back home with him, since I was then completing my year in the Catholic seminary nearby at St. Mary's College in Winona, Minn. On that trip, I recall Marshall watching for the cheapest gasoline on the route and negotiating at a truck stop for fuel to fill his two tanks (perhaps 70 to 80 gallons total). The pump price was 26 cents per gallon or so, and he filled them for 23 cents, after which Marshall and the manager debated the price that had been agreed upon.

Owatonna-35 self-propelled swather

In any case, Dad and I both got a lot of benefit from the new swather. It had a 14-foot "grass head," or cutting bar, which meant it would cut grass and alfalfa as well as grain crops and leave the cuttings in a windrow. Up to then, we used a mower to cut a seven-foot-wide swath of a hay crop, and then a side-delivery rake to whisk the cuttings into a windrow. Windrows of hay are left to dry, then picked up by a hay baling machine or pushed into piles, which are hauled away to make a haystack. Similarly, windrows of grain crops are left in the field until the grain has thoroughly dried and is fit for threshing in a combine or threshing machine. Thus, the new swather markedly reduced hay making labor. It was faster, too, than an older grain swather that we pulled behind a tractor.

Minneapolis Moline Model M tractor

Dad's second purpose in buying the swather was income for my college expenses. We did our own hay and grain fields, of course, then solicited swathing jobs from other farmers in the area. I recall the rate was $1.25 per acre to cut grain, or $1.50 to cut hay or cut in difficult conditions. I got to keep all or most of the receipts, which were something more than $1,000, enough to pay my

International Model 806 diesel

tuition for the year at North Dakota State and more. Together with measuring fields for USDA, working a few weeks for my Uncle Stan, I had most of what I needed for a school year at NDSU.

Advances in machinery were often in half steps. Dad added crop acreage through the years and added machinery to handle the increased field work and keep his sons busy helping with it. By about 1961, we had the DuAll plus two field tractors typical for small farms in the 1950s: A Minneapolis Moline (Model M) gasoline tractor and a Super 88 Oliver diesel row-crop tractor. Both were adequate to pull the size of field machinery we had up to that time – as large as a four-bottom plow, for example.

But the increased acreage meant a need for larger machines. Also, Dad and his brothers sometimes shared machinery. They began expanding to larger tractors and tilling machinery. Dad would need a bigger tractor, for example, to pull a big disk tiller that turned a swath of topsoil 16 feet wide. Until he had a bountiful enough harvest to afford a bigger tractor, he went to his shop and produced a stalwart hitch that allowed the Oliver to hitch up and pull machines in tandem with the Minneapolis. Together, they pulled the 16-foot tiller quite handily. When we cultivated fields together, I was always in front on the Oliver and Dad on the other tractor, where he would control the tilling machinery as well. We tilled a lot of acres that way for a couple of years. But in 1964, Dad was able to buy a new International Harvester 806 diesel tractor. He was 50 years old and that was the first tractor he bought new. It had about 90 horsepower at the drawbar, or nearly the same as the other two tractors combined. Our two-tractor system was gladly retired.

Farm Jobs & Discovery

Some hours on our farm were just pure entertainment: favorite TV shows, playing Monopoly or Tripoli around a table, or pinochle, whist or bridge with my parents and brothers. In the summer, entertainment could mean whisking off to swim at the New England pool, or to a nearby creek or stock dam, especially after a summer cloudburst filled them with fresh water. It could be a visit by one of the similarly large families of cousins or friends, when we played softball, baseball, basketball, or hide and seek, or tried some new mischief.

Most days for a Flying M kid were a blend of chores, daydreaming, reading and study, playing and discovery. Leon had an inventor's knack and passed on a lot of ideas in my early years. One was making guns to shoot rubber bands. Rather than commercial toy versions, he showed us how to cut car and truck tire inner tubes into thin slices. A single-shot pistol could be fashioned from the ends of wooden peach crates. A clothes pin was attached to the handle to hold one end of a stretched band. Then, squeeze the clothespin and zing goes the rubber band. Leon also made a repeater rifle version from a long, thin board, with notches cut along the top. One end of a string was nailed at the front of the notches, then strung along the top so that it dipped into each notch. The bands were stretched from the front of the gun to the notches. Then, pull the string and off go the rubber bands, one at a time or in a hail of flying rubber. We did at least once get into trouble with Dad for rustling an intact or reusable inner tube or two to make ammo for the rubber band guns.

We were cramped into the first old farm house when Leon was staying with us. He decided to bed down on a mattress in an empty bin of the main granary, where the hired man, Bob Grant, also slept in the summer months – at least until fall harvest, when the bins were needed to store grain.

One result of that sleeping arrangement was my first lesson in solar heating. For baths in the old house, we had to haul water into the house in buckets and heat it on a coal stove. But Leon fashioned his own solar shower for summer use. He took a five-gallon fuel can, which had a large opening for filling and a small pouring spout, altered the spout into a sprinkling head and painted the can black so it would absorb maximum solar energy. He would fill the can in the morning and leave it in the sun for the day. It would be warm for his shower when he finished farm work in the evening. He laid a wooden shipping pallet along the back side of the granary, where he could strip down, hang the fuel can above his head and take a shower. Note that Leon went on to excel as a machinist, eventually co-founding L&H Industrial, a huge Wyoming-based service company for all things involving oil rigs and mining machinery. Read a detailed history, *Frontier Industrialists*, free online at *https://goo.gl/5bsKgC*

    I got a scare I wouldn't soon forget when one of our experiments with kerosene lamps went awry in our vacated old house. Brother Joe and I were fashioning bottles and tin cans into rudimentary lamps, and we were perfecting them in a makeshift clubhouse we had in the attic of the old house, which was then used as a chicken coop and for storage. A lighted lamp was accidentally tipped and quickly rolled to the edge of the attic floor and down into the wall of the chicken coup below. Fortunately, we were resourceful. I grabbed the chicken watering fountains just outside the building and handed them to Joe, who poured water down the same segment of the wall were the lamp had gone, dousing the fire. We told Rick about our close call, and he cautioned us, saying sparks from such a fire could hang around in the wall and reignite the fire hours later. Holy smokes! Joe and I took a while to get to sleep that night, peering out our basement bedroom window for any sign of fire at the old house.

    Owing in good part to the access I had to the shop and its mechanical and carpentry tools, acetylene torch, welder and many power tools, our farm was also a great place for inventions and otherwise learning how things work. Inventions were wide ranging. They were often born in a boy's love of fire and explosives, and the actual gains in knowledge came in bits and pieces.

    When I was probably age 10 or older, I found that a small brass fitting for a fuel line turned smoothly onto the end of a 10-inch long steel pipe with about a one-fourth inch inside diameter. The fitting had a small hole at its center, just the right size for a firecracker fuse to stick through. Voila! I was holding the barrel for a homemade pistol. Sixteen-penny nails fit perfectly into the pipe, so I cut a few nails into a half-dozen pieces each with a hacksaw and had some ready ammo. For a tryout, I squeezed my gun barrel in a vice, with the barrel aimed at a shop wall, popped in a 16-penny slug backed by a firecracker, then lit the fuse and ran around a corner.

    Bang! A new dent in the wooden shop wall confirmed my success. To complete the pistol, I bound the barrel to a pistol chassis cut from the end board of a peach crate. My new gun fired if the firecracker wasn't a dud. It was dangerous to life and limb, and somewhat accurate for about 10 feet. My invention did help me see what a challenge it had been for colonial hunters to pack powder and ammo into their muskets before they could get a shot off. And it was easy to see how much easier it was, compared to my do-it-yourself firearm, to just get our .22 rifle from our front hall closet to go hunting.

We also made a few tries at brewing and distilling, likely diversions for boys on a grain farm. One thing prompting our research, beyond basic whiskey distilling information in our Encyclopedia Americana set, was a long piece of copper fuel line needed to cool and condense the evaporated alcohol on its way to our waiting moonshine jug. So Joe and I learned how hard liquor is made. Our product tasted, however, much more like the copper tube than like booze. We found it to be much easier mischief to slip into the root cellar and filch an ounce or two of Grandma Maixner's wine.

On a farm, you get a knack early for handling cars, trucks, tractors and other motorized field machinery. A field is a wonderful classroom because there are usually no objects nearby to hit. At age five or six I would start a truck by pushing the foot pedal starter, ignition switch on and the truck already placed in the lowest gear. I would creep along to where Dad needed the truck and then just turn the switch off. No worries. Driving truck for jobs right in the farmstead, such as driving along the cattle feed bunk while someone in the truck box is shoveling feed, also started as slow-motion driving. Plenty of chances to get familiar with the controls.

Farm driving evolved with age and maturity, so that by about age ten I took short turns with the tractor pulling disc, plow or other soil turning implement, and within another year perhaps, driving trucks on the graveled roads in our township and pulling a rake or other implement in the hay field. By the time I went with Mom to Amidon, the county seat, for my driver's license test, I was comfortable driving, and received a (restricted) license a month before my 14th birthday.

As with driving, other jobs on the farm evolved with maturity and, of course, the strength needed to do them. Our jobs began in preschool years (no kindergarten in those days) with feeding and watering Mom's flock of young chickens and laying hens, picking eggs, hoeing and picking weeds in the garden and potato and sweet corn fields and walking the third of a mile to our mailbox to get the mail. Occasionally in the spring or summer, two or three of us would mix a jar of Kool-Aid or just pack a water jug, and take the wagon to get the mail.

One job for Maixner kids of nearly all ages and parents was to pour a quart of our farm's spring wheat onto the kitchen table and pick out the weed seeds, insect parts and other impurities, preparing it as the next morning's breakfast. A sack of wheat could be kept in the garage or with the sacks of flour in Mom's kitchen flour bin. Like other grains, wheat swells up when cooked in water. Picture Quaker's breakfast cereal called "Puffed Wheat," or think of rice and how it swells when cooked. As a breakfast cereal, the soft, puffed kernels, with a little cream and a sprinkling of sugar, are good to go. Much like oatmeal. Through the fall and winter of some years, if the crops had been ruined by droughts and/or hail, or the markets for wheat or fattened cattle were poor, the budget was tight and we ate wheat for breakfast quite often. Still, I don't believe that I equated it as poverty chow when I sat down to a saucer of cooked wheat. It was just breakfast.

For perhaps two or three years in the late 1950s, it was usually my job to wash the milk separator. The task passed from one sibling to the next, and Rick or Joe subbed in for me during my stint when time conflicts arose. As noted back in the Flying M Critters chapter, this centrifuge machine sat in a room of the milking barn. Its business part is a stainless steel bowl or drum with a stack of about 15 discs inside. Whole milk is spun through the discs, exiting as skim milk and cream. It was fairly laborious to cart the milk-handling parts of the separator to the sink in the utility room of the house, disassemble and clean all parts and reassemble them, and cart the thing back to the milking barn. We all got our turns at washing that damned separator.

Most kid jobs on our farm were just uneventful tasks. But stinky, too, when the task was scooping animal poop from the chicken house, gutter of the milking barn, or calf pens. They were often very dusty and/or gritty, too. Summer fallowing (using a plow or cultivator to turn the soil and kill weeds) on a windy day often meant dirt and sand blowing in the eyes even while wearing a mask to keep the stuff from your sinuses and throat. Perhaps the most disagreeable job in the dusty category was harvesting oats while driving the combine downwind, with the grain's itchy chaff wafting over you.

But the farm jobs also included good laughs and often hatched stories that are retold at family gatherings. Big brother Bill learned about centrifugal force, probably from Leon, by swinging a bucket of water in an upwards circle over his head: If the bucket keeps moving in a speedy circle, inertia keeps the water in the pail. Bill came into the living room of our old house with a tall pail containing the fresh milk or cream from the barn, probably having practiced his trick on the way, and decided to show the trick to Mom. Unfortunately, the tall can hit the ceiling at the top of Bill's swing, stopping the pail momentarily and dumping the milk on the living room floor.

In the new house, Mom got an entire case (12 dozen) of scrambled eggs she hadn't wanted. On typical days we picked perhaps two dozen eggs in the hen house and packed them into cases for family use. The overage was sold to the New England creamery. Some were kept in the kitchen fridge and cases were kept cool in the root cellar. As often happened, Mom accumulated a full case for making a large wedding cake that would need a lot of eggs, and she asked Frank to bring them to the root cellar, where they'd remain cool briefly until baking day.

Unfortunately, Frank, then perhaps 10 years old, missed a step near the top of the full flight into the basement. He and the eggs went flying down the stairs, eggs flying out by the dozen with each tumble. Most of them were broken, plastered on the stairwell, basement floor and Frank. Mom came running down the stairs to see if he was injured, and Frank ran to his bed, pleading for forgiveness for destroying the eggs. Of course, Mom was not pleased one bit that she would have to replace the eggs, but was not planning to punish a kid for falling down the stairs. Frank did face quite a cleaning job, though, with an assist from siblings.

Frank also ends up on the short end of my favorite Flying M slapstick story. We milked from two to four Jersey, Guernsey and Holstein cows through my years on the farm. The first two of those breeds tend toward mild dispositions, while Holsteins are frequently more like moose in both size and surly demeanor. On one spring day, Frank and I went to milk, and I started by feeding the cows their ground oats in their trough in front of them and locking stanchions, which keep them in place while they're milked. Then, because cows produce a lot of sloppy poop when they graze green grass in the spring, I took a scoop shovel and pitched the mushy manure out to the manure pile behind the milking barn. By then, Frank had begun milking a Jersey. I sat down to a rather jumpy Holstein, who started swishing me with her tail and then shifting her hind feet and kicking at the bucket when I tried to draw milk. After some attempts to calm her, she kicked once again and planted her right hind hoof into the milk pail.

Frank, who sat milking the more tranquil Jersey, continued calmly milking the Jersey, and grinned when I got ticked off, grabbed the scoop shovel and swatted the cow a good one on the butt. In reality, a swat only makes a cow more nervous and likely more inclined to kick. But it was a way of settling the score. However, when I took my payback swing, a generous layer of liquid poop in the scoop flew directly into Frank's face. That turned the tables: I was laughing; Frank, not so much. He headed across the yard toward the cattle drink tank to relieve his shit-faced condition, yelling all the way. Mom came running from the house, fearing a tragedy had befallen us.

Mom & the Flying M Kitchen

Mom had duties aplenty in the house, and she kept her outdoor chores to a minimum. She rarely climbed onto a tractor seat or platform or behind the steering wheel of a truck. She did take on a few farm enterprises, though. She ordered the baby chicks and helped get them settled in the chicken house, supervised planting the garden, and the scalding, plucking and processing of chickens on butchering days. But with a husband and eight kids and usually a very tight budget, she was instead focused on housebound tasks. She ordered bolts of fabric and had kid-clothes-making days, usually when we were at school: shirts, dresses and jackets. She even dashed together a few dozen pairs of boxer shorts one year, I recall, using the same pattern from Sears or J.C. Penney and just adjusting it to a range of butt sizes.

Laura Maixner in 1952

In general, Mom's kitchen was set up to feed a hard-working farm family. She designed her cupboards in consultation with our carpenter, Frank Heick. He was not known as a cabinet maker but did a masterful job of it anyway. The doors rode on tracks at top and bottom, and the shelves were deeper at the top than bottom. That way, a maximum of the rather deep countertops were visible and available for cook's work.

Mom's kitchen was a happening place. First of all, it was the primary gathering place. Carcasses of cattle and hogs, already slaughtered and quartered elsewhere, were brought to the big kitchen table for cutting and packaging. Mounds of meat -- pork, beef and sometimes deer and antelope – were ground there or in the garage, and dumped into a big cast iron sausage maker and pressed into the sausage casings. Chickens were processed there and boxed for local delivery or packaged for our freezer.

She developed a broad cooking and baking repertoire. She had Kitchen Aid's biggest home model of mixer with the attendant chopping, grinding and slicing attachments. She picked up a two-gallon deep-fat fryer from the Gardner Hotel restaurant in New England, which had closed. It could fry up pieces from a couple of chickens or french fries from at least a half dozen spuds at once. As one would expect, with plenty red meat and poultry, along with eggs, milk, cream and butter coming from our farm animals, our diets lacked in neither protein nor dairy fat.

Mom kept a couple of 50-pound sacks of bread flour and all-purpose flour in a flip-open bin right beneath the kitchen counter. A batch of bread was usually 12 loaves and might include a couple of cake pans full of caramel rolls or other pastry. Plus, with the big fryer ready to go, some fists of dough were often stretched thin and thrown into the fryer to make dough gods, which we ate hot with sugar or syrup for a quick lunch.

In the late 1950s, we started to pasteurize our milk, giving us another tidbit of knowledge, so I knew about Louis Pasteur before his discovery came up in a high school classroom. The French scientist reported a century earlier how to kill bacteria in milk. By heating it to 161^0 Fahrenheit for a bit, harmful bacteria is destroyed, making the milk safe to drink and greatly delaying it from souring in the fridge. So in the 1950s retail milk was all labeled as "pasteurized." But we got our milk from our own cows, not waxed cartons, and our milking parlor hygiene was off-hand at best. We brushed off bits of weed or dirt from the cow's udder and washed the teats with a pail of water and a rag if they were muddy or had picked up manure. Otherwise, we just sat down and milked straightaway.

So Mom bought a two-gallon pasteurizer, which heated milk to the magical 161 F. It was filled daily, put into cold water to cool and then the fridge to finish cooling. The two gallons were consumed daily for meals and cooking. Cream could also be pasteurized, but most of ours was allowed to sour for churning butter, use in baking, or sale to the New England Creamery. Mom's banana cream pie got real cream-and-lard-based crust.

The carton of eggs that tumbled down the stairs with Frank was one of hundreds that Mom used in her fancy cakes. That enterprise was her main money-maker for many years. She honed her baking and decorating skills and invested in equipment and do-dads needed for an enterprise that brought her personal satisfaction and income. Cakes baked with her repertoire of Lord Baltimore red chocolate cake, for example, and others with almond or lemon filling, were decorated to celebrate marriages, anniversaries, ordinations and more. One was for the banquet celebrating the dedication of our new St. Mary's Church, for example, in 1955. I still run into people from the New England area who say, "Oh, your mom made my wedding cake."

Everyone had a part in Mom's cake business. Dad, for example, soldered a hundred or so metal bottle caps to the heads of 10-penny nails, then drilled rows of holes in short boards to place them vertically. The result was little pedestals on which she extruded frosting to make roses and other sugar flowers to decorate her cakes. Siblings all pitched in with basic assistance to help Mom make her delivery deadlines: breaking dozens of eggs into a bowl, measuring and sifting flour, chopping walnuts, and so forth. The almond nut filling she used between layers in many of her cakes was a favorite for some of us when we snuck into the fridge for a treat. Darcy recalls Mom's challenge in achieving vivid color in making sugar roses, because the liquid red food dyes available then were not intense enough, and adding enough made the frosting too soft to hold its shape. She found a paste dye with intense color that could be stirred into the icing.

Mom developed detailed logistics for transporting her cakes and then decorating them on site. She could finish some cakes in her kitchen, or nearly so, if they were just one-story models to be delivered nearby. But most were two- or three-story architectural challenges, so she had to bake and frost the levels separately, transport them with all the decorations and decorating tools to the delivery site, then put the second and third levels on three- or four-legged pedestals and assemble the high-rise cake and decorate it.

Itinerant vendors of food, farm and household products were a regular feature of mid-20th Century farm life. Top marketers to

farmsteads and rural homes across the country included J.R. Watkins and McConnon's, both based in Winona, Minn., an ideal location for receiving stocks and shipping their products by train on the Northern Pacific. Henry Lee, already well into his years in the 1950s, was our "McConnon Man," and rumbled into our farmstead in his black, windowless panel wagon (picture a Prohibition Era rum-running wagon) a couple of times a year. Mom liked several items peddled by Mr. Lee and the Watkins salesman, who I believe began showing up in my later years on the farm. She favored McConnon's cinnamon, black pepper, almond extract, allspice and nutmeg, Watkins' vanilla and other seasonings that I don't recall.

Those high-flavor items improved the taste of sausages, caramel rolls, Mom's wedding cakes and more. Flying M kids always welcomed Mr. Lee's stops, owing in large part to the McConnon's chewing gum – a freebee – and concentrated sugarless nectar syrup (grape, orange and cherry). You added your own sugar to make a Kool-Aid-type beverage; that way, you mixed it entirely to your taste.

Grandma Luella

Grandma Luella in 1951

In writing about my home town, it makes sense to start with Grandma Luella Maixner, the most important person there in my early life. As I mentioned earlier, we started daily commuting to school near the end of my third grade. Even while still boarding, if one of us became ill, Grandma's house was the place to go until Dad or Mom could get in from the farm. Also, especially in my high school years, activities that kept me after school meant my siblings could leave for home and I'd end up as Grandma's boarder. Same was true when I returned at night from an out-of-town event and my siblings had gone home with the car.

Grandma's house was a wonderful refuge. She knew how to cook, so no one was going to go hungry. But, her heating system was ideal for North Dakota living and loved by her whole family and friends. The furnace in her basement sent heat straight up through a big steel grate in the floor at the center of her dining and living area. So that's where people at her house gathered in cold months.

What's more, Grandma had a second floor with three bedrooms and a bath, plus a bed in a wide hallway landing above the stairwell, so there was always a place to bed down. Even better, through my junior- and senior-high days, she boarded two girls from the public school who were about a year older than me. Also, cousin Jack Wandler, Leon's youngest brother, whom Luella raised, lived there much of the time through his college years. Guys and gals a few years older are always preferred company to a pre-teen or teenager and a good source for learning some of the tricks of teenager survival.

But those weren't the only fringe benefits of having Luella as my Grandma. She had attended schools in her hometown, Owatonna,

Minn., before marrying Vendelin (John) in about 1910 and soon joining him on his farming claim. She educated herself well over the years as a naturalist, gardener and general household manager. For example, while John farmed, one of her sidelines flourished: raising and marketing a flock of turkeys. The enterprise went a long ways toward keeping her family afloat through the economically harsh 1930s and may have provided the spark for Mom's chicken enterprise.

Grandpa John was, unfortunately, crippled by strokes in the 1940s, and a stroke killed him in late 1948. Luella bought a house and retired in New England in 1950 and brought her green thumb to town. Her neighbors were as jealous of her wonderfully diverse and flourishing garden in New England as her clan was delighted in the tasty foods coming from it. Not just a vegetable garden on her New England lot, but also apple trees, a flower garden and sundry other plots and pots of flowering plants, and patches of raspberries and strawberries. Her Chevy had to share half of her garage with a mushroom bed.

While I learned a lot about animals and field crops on the farm, I picked up a few things from Grandma as well. My siblings and I often mowed her lawn with a push mower, helped to weed the garden, plant veggies and flowers and so forth. When the tasks were finished, we often got quarters from a little pottery piece, fronted with a Dutch boy and girl, that I still keep above my desk.

Grandma's coin box

I picked up bits of gardening wisdom from her. One day in late spring when pulling weeds in her long strawberry patch, I carefully patted the soil around the roots of new seedlings that we were adding there. She, on the other hand, gathered a bunch of seedlings in her apron, chopped a small hole in the soil with her hoe, plopped a seedling into it, stomped it to firm into place, and explained to me that strawberries are not timid plants and would grow well in any soil where they felt welcome. Subsequent weeks proved her right about those strawberry seedlings.

Another time, I was pulling weeds in her vegetable garden and didn't want to pull up valued plants, so I asked her which ones are the weeds. "A weed is just a plant growing where you don't want it to grow," she explained. To a seven-year-old, that was profound.

Her green thumb found its way to our farm and those of other family members. She had colonies of honey bees in or bordering our alfalfa fields, which usually peppered with volunteer clover plants. We helped her manage the hives and harvest (and consume) the honey. She made a variety of wines with berries, other fruit and rhubarb. We went chokecherry picking with her to collect the grist for wine and jam.

Luella was a prayerful, thoughtful woman, whose reading included time with her Bible before retiring at night. I think she had an out-sized influence on me because overnight stays with her were not television nights, but often reading, visiting, doing homework and such while seated over her furnace grate. She braided huge, colorful rugs, her wintertime avocation, while sitting at her furnace grate, and we sometimes helped tear and cut rags and other cloth into strips that would become braided rag rope and then rug. She did one each year as a Lenten project. The result was plenty of time with Grandma Luella. So while my parents were raising eight kids at once, visits with grandma were often one on one.

Luella had a powerful presence. She was no wilting violet when it came to giving directions or asserting her views within the family, parish or town, and her strong, high-pitched voice ensured that people noticed when she spoke up. I still recall the quiet afternoon in my third grade classroom with Sister Mary Miles when the door popped open about a foot and Grandma's voice thundered through the room. "Is Eddie Maixner in here?" I was startled and embarrassed, but the teacher just calmly told me to attend to Grandma, who waited in the hall and gave me a bag to bring home to Mom.

In the same third-grade classroom, I was also flustered when Joyce Wanner, a pleasant, soft-spoken classmate and I were listed to take our turns with after-school classroom sweeping and dusting. I had the boys' job of sweeping the room, which included getting down on knees and sweeping under the rows of desks with a little hand brush. As I was finishing a row, I heard Joyce's voice above me, "Do you want a kiss?" I did not look up immediately. "Huh?" But when I did look up, she was holding a Hershey's chocolate kiss.

Grandma drilled a few basic lessons of courtesy into me. If she offered me a cup of tea or a sweet, for example, two responses were appropriate: "Yes, please," or "No, thank you." One learned quickly that responses such as, "I suppose," or, "OK," were those of an ingrate or uncultured person.

Luella was especially big on affirming people and withholding judgments against others, and she was hell on gossiping. We were Roman Catholics, and if she smelled discrimination against other races or Christian sects, her voice would jump an octave or so and she would bark: "The idea!" She condemned talk that was snide or criticized others. She would remind us to be proud of ourselves and not to slouch, but she told me to remember that I wasn't "one cocky comment better than the next guy." When Luella picked flowers and made bouquets for the altar at St. Mary's Catholic Church, she made enough so that she and her friends also delivered bouquets to the Our Redeemer Lutheran, First Congregational and the Assembly of God churches as well.

Luella's black 1953 Chevy was restored in blue, thanks to cousin Jack Wandler.

Luella's black '53 Chevy made at least one trip that, shall we say, was less sanctified than her deliveries of altar flowers, I learned recently. (Actually though, with Jack, handsome and single and often on the move with her car, perhaps there were other unholy trips as well.) In any case, she, like many other North Dakotans then, left her keys in her car. Her boarders, Claudia Rustan (Dolecheck) and Darlys Thielman (Bentz), one day after supper decided to drive around a bit with Grandma's Chevy.

Without asking her okay, Claudia recalls, they picked up a pal, Arlene Bohlman, and decided to "cruise Dickinson," the happening town a half hour north of New England. "We were probably looking for boys ... got a burger ... got back to town a little late, so we stayed up all night long," she reported. "We even put gas in the car so it wouldn't look like it was driven," she said. But, back at Grandma's, they felt guilty and caved quickly. "She didn't get a chance to call our bluff because we spilled our guts about the whole night," Claudia said. The joyriders ended up talking with their Congregational Church pastor about their wayward trip. Plus, "we had our parents come in, and we all met with Grandma. She just shook her head. Nothing more was needed for punishment." Claudia's epilogue: "She made the best poppy seed rolls. But yes, she kept us in line."

A Throng of Teachers, Young and Old

Since I grew up on a farm eight miles from the nearest town, a lot of my learning came in the course of chores, experimentation in the farm shop, observing plants and animals and what happened in the fields, pastures, creeks and sky. So I wasn't, for example, big on collecting and trading professional baseball cards, a popular diversion with my town friends. (I saved a small bundle of Detroit Tigers ones and was a fan mostly because I liked tigers.) But I could tell you that prairie crocuses blossomed on hilltops about a week after the frost was out of the topsoil, which was when we started to plant spring wheat. And my life was far from isolated, considering the presence of my family, regular visits by extended family and an array of interesting neighbors, and the daily flow of information from our mailbox, radios and television set.

My parents valued news highly. Mom pored through fiction and non-fiction books. Dad had attended only grade school as a kid and was, like me, a plodding reader. But they both had big appetites for world, national and local news and, despite a modest budget, kept a stream of newspapers and news magazines landing in our mailbox and onto our kitchen table. Over the years, they included *Newsweek, Time, U.S. News & World Report, Life, Look*, and more. Also, the arrival of our first black-and-white-screened TV in 1957 brought us the Huntley-Brinkley Report, NBC's televised evening news. So news was a large slice of Flying M life, read and discussed in the kitchen, truck cabs in the field, and on the road in our station wagon.

My bed area was always graced with news, *Mad* magazines and other mags, comic books, etc., to keep abreast of pop culture, politics, Hollywood happenings, and such, also supplying fodder for school assignments. Dad and, once again, Frank Heick build bedrooms in the basement, an upgrade from the boys' dorm, in about 1958. After Bill left for college in the fall of 1960, Rick moved into his room, and I scored my own bedroom around the time I reached high school.

My parents' attention to news blended with an emphasis on public policy and participation in local and state government. When I was growing up, they had little time for big-screen politics but were active in things like township management and the local Farmers Union co-op. Once us kids were into our teens and beyond, they waded in farther. Dad ran unsuccessfully a couple of times in mid- and late-1960s for the North Dakota House of Representatives as a Democrat in our rock-rib-Republican District 39, and then ran once for the state Senate in the early 1970s.

Eventually, Rick, who had married and returned to begin farming around 1970, made the effort and was elected to the House in 1976, then later to the Senate. Mom never ran for public office, but the state Democratic women elected her as vice president, and later as president, in the 1970s. She was appointed by Democratic governors to several statewide panels, including the Social Services Board, the Humanities Council and the Educational Broadcasting Council.

Still, while politics, money and religion are increasingly important as a kid matures, few things are more important than keeping up with your peers – ahead of them if you're lucky. Being cool. Being liked. Staying ahead of the pack where you can. I got a lot of cues daily by listening to Bill and Rick on how to play my hand at life. While I was a bit tardy in maturing physically, they were both good students, each about 6-foot-3-inches tall and athletic. Rick succeeded as the varsity heavyweight wrestler, and he was the guy who got me into playing drums for our rock band. Hard to beat a brother like that, though I was not particularly appreciative at the time. I mean, he was often grouchy and sometimes whacked me if I ticked him off.

Cousins can be a blessing, too, and I had a throng of wonderful ones. Dad had eight siblings, Mom had four, and I ended up with nearly 40 first cousins on Dad's side and a dozen on Mom's. Some were a lot older than me, and some lived in other parts of the country. But we had a bevy of them close by, too, and our basement recreation room was filled with kids when the Jacobs cousins visited. We also had a favorite place to romp in the big dairy barn's hay loft at the Jacobs farm when we visited there. Barb, the oldest, was just a month younger than me, and we became trusting lifelong pals. Boys at St. Mary's hung out mostly with boys; girls, with girls. But I knew I had the closest thing to a sister in my classroom. We practiced the basics of rock and roll dancing – jitterbug – together in the eighth grade, when I would have been embarrassed to try it with most others. When I decided to try out the Catholic seminary after high school, Barb decided to try the convent with the School Sisters of Notre Dame, the order serving our school.

Barb, 5th grade

Some of the older cousins were a treasure for me as well. They included the Wolff sisters, my older big-city cousins in Bismarck. Jeannette, the youngest but around seven years older than me, was devoted to scouting and took me hiking sometimes in Bismarck, on our buttes, and elsewhere. She coached me in current affairs and social mores, and more. I recall LaVyrl, who had finished high school and gotten a job, also started showing up to visit our farm in a sporty two-door hardtop Buick. She helped improve my jitterbug as well.

LaVryl helped close the book on our household's belief in Santa Claus. On a pre-Christmas visit in December 1959, Darcy, the youngest and nearly six years old, enticed her to our parents' bedroom to share a secret. She led LaVyrl to their long closet and pulled out the tail of a Santa Claus jacket at the far end of the rack, whispering, "look what we have to surprise the little kids at Christmas." At that point, with no one littler in the house, LaVyrl expected she wasn't spilling the beans by sharing the mirth of the moment.

I'll step back a generation here to salute a wonderful cast of uncles and aunts – both Dad's and Mom's siblings. Barb's dad, Walter Phillip Jacobs, was my second-to-youngest uncle and was a high-energy guy. He married Dad's youngest sister, Luella (Lu), and they started farming and having babies and kept at it until they had ten (children, not farms). Walt was a natural story teller. He also had a repertoire of pencil cartoons. I recall learning from him very early how to draw "Kilroy Was Here," the cartoon face of a bald man with a big schnoz peering over a board fence. The image was drawn by thousands of U.S. soldiers in World War II to leave a message that they had been there. Walt drove an Army truck in Europe in WWII, and he often planted a Kilroy in his drawings.

Walt loved drawing outhouses. Note the Rainy Buttes on the horizon.

Behind the wheel, Walt had a heavy foot, so the state highway patrol and other cops in the area knew him as a speedster. He regaled family and friends with humorous accounts of stops for traffic violations. Such tales were sort of patterned after Road Runner & Wile E. Coyote cartoons, and featured himself as the one getting snatched up by wily Patrolman Ken Bates, who was assigned to our patrol district in 1959. Bates liked his job and enjoyed knowing the territory and the people, so he passed up promotions and remained our resident highway bull until his retirement in 1988. On one winter evening, Bates took up a position along the main highway near the edge of Bowman, his home town, while traffic was pouring in for a Christmas holidays basketball tournament. Walt was signaled to stop. At the side of the highway, with dozens of basketball fans, including both Bates' and Walt's friends and neighbors, driving by, Walt hopped out and stood with his hands high in the air, grinning at the crowd. "Walt, put your hands down, for god's sake," Bates told him (according to Walt anyway).

Walt Jacobs

Walt moved from his farm into New England in 1983 and, nearing age 60, began to slow down on farm work. My brother Joe was managing the New England Cenex service at the time and tried to help by slowing Walt's highway speed as well. He asked one of the mechanics there to bond a chunk of 2-by-4 board beneath his car's gas pedal. That intrusion did the job for one trip across New England. Walt appreciated Joe's concern and laughed while he removed the cruising impediment.

Walt's father, J.Q. Jacobs, a native of Holland, was a regional leader in the North Dakota Nonpartisan League after World War II. The NPL was a populist branch of the state's Republican Party, born as a farmers' revolt during World War I. It took over the party in 1919 and remained a strong part of the state GOP for about 40 years. So Walt was also an NPLer.

Until March 29, 1956, that is. On that date, the 170 delegates to the NPL convention in Bismarck voted to leave the Republican Party and merge with the Democrats, forming the Democratic-NPL Party (its name yet today). The delegates to the NPL convention made plans to join the delegates to the Democratic state convention, which was to meet in Bismarck a few days later. Stan was a Democratic delegate at that convention. Walt Jacobs, meanwhile, was an NPL delegate in Bismarck, and he joined the others walking into the Democratic convention, where the party had agreed to award half of the state's delegate seats at the national Democratic convention to NPL members. Brother Rick reports: "As they walked in, banners and signs waving, Walt saw Stan sitting with an empty chair beside him so he slipped in next to him" in the delegate seating, thus providing a kind of family demonstration of the two political parties' unification.

Dad and Uncles Walt and Stan were all active in local Democratic politics, Farmers Union and so forth, and they all ran for the House of Representatives in some years. Stan was elected for one term in 1964. Our legislative district was staunchly Republican but he was carried in that year with a national Democratic landslide election.

Another talented story teller was my Uncle Bob Steckman, my Mom's younger brother. He and his wife, Joan, lived in Omaha, so we didn't see him as often as we saw Dad's farming family. But we looked forward to his visits, which included annual trips in October to hunt pheasants. In one yarn, Joan was driving a camper pickup, returning on a highway into Omaha in heavy traffic and with a couple of kids in the cab with her. Bob was rolled up in a blanket on the bench in the back when a stoplight forced Joan to brake hard at a very busy highway intersection, dumping Bob onto the camper floor behind. But just as Bob stepped out, wearing only his underwear and a blanket, to see what was going on, the light turned green and Joan took off, leaving Bob standing in the intersection. A city cop picked Bob up and drove him home, taking a shorter, faster route than Joan's. Bob had his blanket and shorts but no key, so he waited for Joan on the front steps. She saw Bob standing up on the steps as she headed up the driveway and drove straight into the garage door. Anyway, that's how Bob told it.

Increasingly, landowners in Rainy Butte Township posted "No Hunting" signs to ban hunting without the landowner's permission, especially during autumn seasons for deer and antelope, pheasants and other upland birds. So the signs were not welcomed when we went pheasant hunting with Bob. I think it was Rick who asked: "Uncle Bob, if you saw the biggest-ever cock pheasant sitting on top of a No Hunting sign, what would you do?" Bob said: "First I'd shoot the pheasant and then the sign."

One seeming detail of Bob's visits left me a lasting lesson. Bob's and Joan's kids were several years younger than me, and I was enough older than them that I was observing ways parenting was done, instead of just being a kid taking orders. Bob had what I thought was a simple but effective tool for discipline, which he called "a thunk on the head." If a kid failed to comply with an order, there was a warning of a thunk and then, if needed, he would form a fist and flick one finger out to administer a tap on the top of the head. My first thought back then was: That isn't much of a punishment, especially compared with the "Fanny Whacker" that hung above our kitchen table. But then I thunked my own head and found that, yes, it does sting. Still, the penalty, like the threat of a swat from our Fanny Whacker, was primarily psychological: mostly the pain of disapproval, not physical pain.

Through my early childhood, we had a dozen farmsteads within about a mile and a half of our house, but I saw the farmer ranks steadily thin out, owing to deaths and retirements of old timers and with others selling out and moving to cities. In the course of that, a constant was Walt and Margaret Anderson, who were about a decade older than my parents and were as close to us as our relatives. They were at our kitchen table as frequently as any relative. They had raised their children in Milwaukee and then began returning each spring through summer to run a modest farm on the opposite side of Old Baldy from our farmstead.

Walt often hired himself and his grain combine out to Dad at harvest, for example, when he had his own harvesting in hand. His first occupation was as a machinist, and he was generous in repairing parts or building tools in his shop for our operations and for others. When I was in my twenties, I purchased a power drill with a quarter-inch chuck, which meant I could use bits no larger than 0.25 inch diameter. Bless his soul, instead of suggesting I get a drill to accommodate my set of bits, Walt took the bits to his lathe and turned all of the larger ones down to a quarter inch so they fit in my drill's chuck. Talk about above and beyond. He was also a good welder and general mechanic, and he helped Dad, my brothers and me with countless repairs and machinery alternations.

The Andersons were trusted neighbors, friends and ardent Farmers Union members.

Walt and Margaret were both active labor union members to the core. In fact, Margaret, a Wisconsin native, was a leader in organizing the women's garment makers union in Milwaukee. She faced down factory owners' thugs and lines of cops with her compatriots, striking for the right to form a union and for better pay and hours. Walt and I discussed local, state and national political news often, but we as often joked and talked about farming.

Unfortunately, Walt had the very perilous fault of driving at high speeds on our narrow country roads and often stayed near the middle going over hilltops. When growing up and learning to drive, we were advised of Walt's driving habits and often referred to him as the "Flying Swede," because of both his speed and his sometimes unleashed liberal political views. We reminded each other when driving to approach the top of a hill in anticipation that Walt was coming on the other side. Long after I left the farm, when he was quite aged, he severely injured himself going headlong into a neighbor's car at a hilltop. He never fully recovered and died not too long after his accident.

A closing note about Walt is about his leaving keys in his cars. Policy on most farms in our area was to keep keys in the ignition switch of trucks and other farm machines, and in cars, too, though most folks would pull them from cars when the family left for a trip. The policy rarely fostered thefts of vehicles and meant that a truck could be used when needed, without the driver having to locate whomever took the key. But when Andersons left their farmstead to winter in Milwaukee, Walt always left the keys in one car or pickup. He thought about people possibly stranded in the usually harsh winter conditions there, and said of his car: "What if somebody needs it?"

Home Town

View of New England from a hilltop northeast of the town

New England was eight road miles from our farmstead and across the county line in Hettinger County. It began as a prairie boom town. The Milwaukee Road, now operated as the Canadian Pacific Railway's Soo Line, began serving there in 1910. For decades, nearby farmers rapidly expanded harvests of wheat, barley and other grain. Grain elevators went up lickety-split there, and by 1947 New England was acclaimed to be the largest primary grain market in the world.

In 1950, the town's main street was fully lighted. Most of its streets were paved by the time I entered grade school, and the place had a robust array of businesses to serve its 1,100 or so residents, plus at least triple that population from the area's farms. Today, just a few grain merchants operate on what we called "Elevator Row," and the town has fewer than 600 residents.

I think the following little event reflects New England's personality. Brother Bill told of one of this friends driving a big farm truck down Main Street in the daytime, with an elderly lady approaching in her car from the opposite direction. Without signaling, she turned in front of the truck, resulting in a fender bender but no injuries. The truck operator got out to check on the lady and his truck and said, "you didn't give me a signal for your turn." Replied the old lady: "But I always turn here. Everybody knows that."

Just a few of New England's once long stretch of elevators still operate today.

My guess is that Gerry Bargman, the town cop during my high school years and after, did due diligence and filed a report for the insurance carriers but didn't issue a traffic citation.

Bargman was a decent guy, trying to watch over New England folks and help them while patrolling the place without unnecessary public commotion. The right sort of cop for a small-town, though he did generate a few Gerry-the-cop tales. Grandma Luella also acknowledged that she had earned a citation for not signaling for a left turn, probably during Gerry's initial months as cop there, when he was trying to impress the town council that he was taking police duties seriously. Family members have related her comment about the ticket: "Oh, the damned fool," she said of the new cop and his unnecessary ticket. That's life in a small town, for sure.

One day, Gerry observed a sedan moving slowly down a street ahead of him, but doing so without a driver: No heads protruded above the seats. Alarmed, he sped ahead of the runaway car far enough to stop his patrol car and race to fling open the driver's door of the other vehicle and jump behind the wheel. But as he leapt into the car, he found himself in the lap of Marjorie Walch. Gerry hadn't been able to see her from behind, but Marjorie, though something under five feet tall, was just going about her business and was able to see out of her car well enough to get where she was going.

Besides a very busy Rexall Drug Store, several car, truck and farm equipment dealerships, a lumberyard, a couple of grocery stores and auto service stations, a blacksmith, and more, the biggest business in New England was grain: a row of seven or more big grain elevators did a huge business in buying and shipping grain, cleaning it to sell as seed, selling fertilizer and field chemicals and so forth. New England supported about the same number of taverns, including the Golden West. That bar was, in general, the favorite among my relatives and was owned and operated by the parents of my

Among the Golden West's most avid pinochle, whist and rummy players of the '50s and '60s: Corny Schmitt (left) and Frank (center) and Louie Reisenauer

pal, Calvin Steiner. I stayed over some nights in his family's apartment over the bar and sometimes helped Cal sweep up the bar or do other tavern cleaning and odd jobs.

For the Maixner siblings, New England was where we headed at the end of many a hot summer day to reach the swimming pool before it closed, especially on Saturdays, when the family would then hang around town with friends for the evening. The town was our primary market. Besides the meats, milk and cream, vegetables and other foods produced on our farm, Mom often stocked up at supermarkets in Dickinson or Bismarck, especially for fruit or veggies to can or freeze. But New England stores were crucial to the Flying M, especially for fuel, farm supplies, machinery parts and service, and more.

The Rexall was essential for medicines for our family and livestock, but was also usually the top spot for treats, school supplies, and comic books. The latter were an important part of life for most grade school boys in the 1950s and early 1960s, an era when television programming was still quite limited, and it was long before the internet. The Rexall had a generous stock of comic books in open shelves behind the checkout desk. What's more, the owner, Al Hammes, and later, Emil Zueger, both had a pretty tolerant policy for kids (mostly boys) who wanted to sit next to the counter and read comic books without buying them. Put them back in place without damaging them and you were usually free of reprimands or demands to buy comic books. Some were able to read most of their favorites without buying, or buying very few. I wasn't very aggressive about it, but did page through some *Archie, Donald Duck* and *Superman* comic books and *Mad* magazines without cost.

On the farm, we had a single wide-tired, one-speed bike that was already well used when we got it. But when I was about eight years old we won a nifty two-speed Columbia bike (years before ten-speed ones became popular). It was the top annual prize awarded by the Rexall store and was given to kids for whom shoppers credited the most dollars in purchases (not to the kids who themselves bought the most). Note that Mom and Mrs. Hammes, the owner's wife, were very close friends, so some unwarranted collusion may have won us the bike.

Since I was a farm kid, I was able to join in my New England peers' shenanigans only occasionally. One antic was what might be called the Roman candle bombardment. When July 4th approached and fireworks were sold, boys would buy some Roman candles: Tubes that shoot an intermittent series of colored, sparkling fireballs about 50 to 100 feet in whatever direction the candle is pointed. Some of them were snitched from family July 4th supplies. The idea was to hide behind bushes along Main Street, plant the candle so the fireballs would hit or streak near cars and trucks coming down the street, then light one as vehicles approached. Next move, of course, was to high-tail it for a block or two in another direction once the show was under way.

Halloween in New England, as elsewhere, is a traditional evening for kids' mischief. In New England, we did the traditional door-to-door trick-or-treating on Oct. 31st, which often included a few tricks to impress your friends and/or irritate home and business owners. But also, as in some other towns across the U.S. and Canada, in many years we unleashed an evening of trickery and pubic disruption on Oct. 30. It is variously called Mischief Night, Devil's Night, or Gate Night, with the latter name owing to the custom of removing yard gates and leaving them in neighboring yards or elsewhere. New England called it Gate Night. It was a farming community, and we moved the things that were there. It meant opening gates to farm dealership lots and pulling machinery into the street, or moving other cars, trucks or tractors into the streets.

The Maixner kids were sometimes in New England on Halloween night. Most of the kids knew Grandma Luella, who made a huge pan of popcorn balls and left it out on her back porch with the light on there and a hand written sign inviting visitors to take one. I helped her make them at least a couple of times. Grandma Maixner inspired a sense of decorum, and most kids just took one and moved along.

Although I did end up in town on Gate Night in perhaps a couple of my pre-teen and teen years, my parents were not about to haul a load of children into their home town for mischief night. So, in most years, I just saw the aftermath when, for example, we would drive in for mass on Sunday morning, or to school, and see farm implements, equipment trailers, grain elevators and such from the machinery lot next door sitting in the street next to St. Mary's Church.

Thus, I missed out on one bit of chicanery that occurred on Gate Night of 1964 and is imbedded in New England history. The 30-foot metal flagpole on the front lawn of the public school had been newly repainted and was standing loosely in its sleeve in the ground. Three of my compatriots – Bob Gardner, Rick Brentrup, and Dan Juelfs – plus a couple of guys a few years older, managed to lift it out and drop it to the ground. But it landed with a big bang, which made the older two nervous about being seen, so they split.

But soon the trio went to work. They got a badly damaged, windowless pickup truck owned by Gardner's dad, and stuck the pole through the rear window and windshield openings. Then, with Rick and Dan balancing it precariously, carried it through darkened streets across town. The adventure included a madcap ride, with the pole rolling back and forth and sticking out more than 20 feet in front of the pickup as Bob drove. To avoid discovery, the crew even headed out on a darkened Highway 22 for a ways at the town's edge. They toted it to Doc Brown's Park, a little playground area near city hall, dug a posthole there and replanted the pole. Gerry the cop showed up and shined a light on their endeavor just as they were tamping dirt to firm up the flagpole in its new home. Anyway, the punchline was delivered by Gerry the cop when he told folks in the bowling alley that evening that he saw kids messing around with the flagpole in Doc Brown's Park and had even bent it over. He wondered just what they were trying to do with the park's flag pole (not realizing that the park wasn't supposed to have a flag pole).

The Decoys, the rock and roll band in which I played during my last three years of high school, blended Flying M, home town and school activities. Brother Rick (base) lead the endeavor, and classmates Gene Paul (lead guitar) and Vern Meyer (brass), plus Roger Hanson, a friend of Gene's (rhythm and lead singer), joined up. That left the band in need of a drummer, and I was recruited. With perhaps two months of practice, I was deemed adequate to provide a beat. The band was a lot of fun. It meant gigs playing in several southwestern North Dakota towns (plus a dance at St. Mary's High School) and traveling with older guys. The band was likely a factor in getting me dates with girls I might not otherwise have landed. Who knows.

Our first gig had a nearly disastrous outcome. We played for a dance at the Gascoyne community hall and learned a lesson about combining alcohol and musical performance. We all had dates. Someone had secured beer for us and, since we were all high school kids, our tolerance for alcohol was minimal. By the time we started playing, we sounded terrible and weren't even delivering a good dance beat. So we announced an unscheduled break, and Rick had us all walking around outside in the cold, gulping coffee, trying to get our heads on straight. Back on stage, we did better, which isn't saying much, but we got through the night. After that, dates on performance nights were more occasional, and alcohol in any form was verboten until after the last tap of the tom-tom. We did not, however, get another invitation to play at Gascoyne.

Three Decoys members headed for college at the end of summer after my sophomore year, so the Decoys were dormant through most of the next two school years, though we did manage a few appearances during holiday breaks and summers for a couple more years. We did a lot of purely instrumental songs by the Ventures, favorites by Buddy Holly, Elvis Presley, Roy Orbison, early Beatles and Rolling Stones, and some other high energy instrumental pieces such as the Surfaris' "Wipe Out," and Boots Randolph's Yakety Sax.

We needed a place to jam and that place was usually the Flying M basement rec room. Considering the roof-flapping decibels involved, practices were often set for when my parents were away from the farmhouse, but not always. They put up with the racket sometimes. Mom's attitude was that she would rather we play in our basement than were out drinking and jamming at another locations and then driving home. My training in music was limited and episodic, though I sang in school choruses and choirs through high school. I took piano lessons in second and third grades, played the drums until the noise they produced in the basement music room during my year in the seminary was not appreciated. So I traded the drums for a nice Gibson acoustic guitar.

School Days

St. Mary's Church in recent times; former high school building is to the right.

Attending grade and high school years at St. Mary's School in New England was a huge part of my childhood. I started first grade a month short of my sixth birthday and boarded Monday through Friday until the spring of third grade. My boarding years went fairly well despite my tender years. With older brothers Bill and Rick also at St. Mary's, and Grandma Luella just a 10-minute walk from school, I had excellent backstops. Further, I had already acquired my cousin Barb Jacobs along with Bob Gardner and Rick Brentrup as pals because our families were friends. Plus my parents would sometimes stop by mid-week if they were in town. I think I felt lonely only occasionally when things weren't going my way.

For me and many of my rural peers, the need to board receded because older siblings were getting driver's licenses and roads were being improved rapidly throughout Slope and Hettinger counties, making daily commuting feasible, and, in time, easy.

I recall just a few traumatic moments. My first grade teacher, Sister Madeleva, invited us to bring a Christmas gift to school when we returned after the New Year for a show and tell. I don´t recall what toy I brought. But Dennis Kohl brought a big red metal fire engine. I can't say for sure if he had given me an okay to play with it in the classroom, but I headed out into the snow with it and lost one of the nuts that secured the front wheels. Then I frost-bit my fingers trying to find it in the snow. As punishment for absconding with Dennis' truck, I had to return after dinner and stand in a corner of the classroom for an hour with my frost bit fingers.

Another time, in the second grade, I believe it was, I did something that offended a classmate, and a bunch of kids ganged up and had me cornered in a school basement window well and started to throw things at me. At that moment, Victor Roller came by. Victor was several years older and had missed a couple of grades in school, but was revered as a very tough guy. Plus the Rollers were good family friends: A big family with eight boys and a girl who lived just a few miles north of our farm. Victor asked who was in the window well. Then, learning that it was me, he declared: "You leave Eddie Maixner alone," and the crowd dispersed.

One of the rare actual spankings I recall getting from Dad was for misbehaving in the boys' dormitory. The dorm was in the basement of the grade school, an old department store building that had been refashioned into a school house. There were rows of single and double beds. Brothers shared double beds, so Joe and I shared a bed.

On winter nights, we often heard the heating system pipes clanking overhead in the hallway and the nearby furnace room. We had a prayer together and lights went out, then everyone was supposed to be quiet and go to sleep, though a little whispering in the beds and between beds was usual. Nuns would take turns as dorm prefects. One night after lights out and the supervising nun had left, I started teasing and taunting kids in surrounding beds and topped it off by jumping on the bed while chanting something about Kenny Reisenauer, the boy across the aisle from our bed, having raisins for brains. That is, until I lost my spot in space over the bed and landed loudly on the floor. Dang! One of the nuns came marching in, and before the week was out there was a phone call or note going from St. Mary's to the Flying M.

I learned years later that Mom had instructed Dad that spankings were in order. So Joe and I got a short oral examination in the kitchen when we arrived home on Friday afternoon, then Dad said that I needed a spanking. "Damn outlaws of the dorm," he declared, swung me over his lap, gave me a few hard swats, and then repeated the ritual with Joe. I had been the ringleader. Joe hadn't done much of anything wrong; likely not even jump on the bed.

When our school commuting days began in the spring of 1956, our township roads to our farmstead had been newly improved and graveled, and the weather was warming, making travel easier. Bill was set to have his driver's license by the start of the next school year, his freshman year, and began escorting Rick, me, Joe, Fran and Frank to school in a 1950 Dodge, which I think Dad bought from Grandpa George Steckman. Grandpa had started buying a few cars to gussy up and resell in his very brief retirement before he died. There would have been no votes in our family against daily commuting. My parents appreciated losing the cost of boarding us, plus we helped with both morning and evening chores in the feedlot, milking barn, hen house, etc. We liked getting home to Mom's cooking at night, our own beds, television in the basement family room, etc.

On school commuting days, we would be up by 7 a.m., or perhaps 6:30 if we were going to mass before school. We would do chores assigned before school, get dressed and pile into the Dodge by 8 a.m., or by perhaps 7 a.m. if any of us were to serve at mass. Serving at mass meant, of course, that anyone else heading to the school and church had to arrive early as well. It also meant that anyone beyond the second grade (when we took our first communion) had to fast in the morning until after mass. On church mornings, we could have a glass of milk before leaving home, but had to bring along something to eat for breakfast after mass. (The required Catholic fast before communion was relaxed somewhat in about 1960, allowing one to eat solid foods up to three hours, and drink beverages up to one hour, before receiving the Eucharist.)

Though there were eight Maixner kids, our school car, the Dodge, and later a 1953 Chevy Bel Air, maxed out at seven school-bound Maixners. Not all eight of us at once, since Bill finished high school a few months before Darcy started first grade (no kindergarten at that time).

Since older siblings in the many farming families in

The model of car I drove to school: '53 Chevy Bel Air

areas west of New England were driving their siblings, often with other neighboring kids, we waved and honked to cars on ND Highway 21. One morning's trip to school left a horrible Highway 21 memory. Less than two miles from school, we came upon a car with kids from three families that had just had a head-on collision with a car driven by an elderly woman who may have had a heart attack or stroke, and whose car had come over a hill directly in their path. When we stopped at the smash up, a few other travelers were pulling kids from the wreckage. Kids were screaming and moaning and I saw some bleeding. Two girls in my class had been riding in the front seat, and Philomena Reisenauer been killed. Another, Darlene Koffler (Meier), was badly injured but eventually recovered. We continued on to school, and I entered my freshman homeroom just as Sister Kenneth had called the classroom to order for the day, unaware of the tragedy. I informed the class about what had happened. Such times one doesn't forget.

In the 1960s, North Dakota let kids get driver's learning permits and restricted driver's licenses by about 14 years of age. Rick was more than two years older than me, so he drove us to school most days until the fall of 1963, when Rick had finished high school and I was at the wheel with five siblings. One constant in the commuting operation was young siblings having to wait for older ones to finish sports practice or other after school events. In the fall, fortunately for me, I commonly had my own junior varsity football practices while Bill and Rick had their varsity practice, and I had basketball practice while Rick wrestled.

We could visit with friends or play outdoors around the school grounds after classes, of course, but soon only younger siblings of varsity athletes remained, and the default activity was study hall in the top bleachers of the school gymnasium. I had lots of hours in that unofficial study hall, as did all of my younger siblings. The consolation, of course, was that doing homework in the bleachers meant much less to do at home. But the routine varied. I was out of sports during my junior year owing to an injury, so I suppose I often waited for younger siblings to finish their after-school activities that year.

When I was going to North Dakota State and returning home summers, Dad had picked up a 1951 Ford from neighboring farmer Frank Reisenauer. It ran OK but was the drabbest faded blue gray ever. Plus we found its horn didn't work. To make the car presentable to Frank's friends, we spray painted it cherry red with three white racing stripes over the top, bumper to bumper. We borrowed a big, loud horn from a truck and mounted it right in the middle of the engine hood, more than satisfying the legal requirement for a working horn. So that is what Frank, Fran, Laura Lu and Darcy took to school. Frank, who was doing most of the school driving, said it worked well enough but got more than its share of attention from Gerry the cop.

One day Gerry pulled him over because he and his friends were doing some vehicular shenanigan. A low profile cop, he told Frank that he would tell his dad if he had reason to stop him again. But the warning had extra implications. Fran is Frank's twin and was also licensed to drive. But this was in an era when guys did the guys' things like driving – well before Title IX amendments to the 1972 Education Act, which soon prompted equal participation in athletics for girls. Frank was a varsity football and basketball player and had a reputation to uphold. So he would have been ultra-embarrassed if Gerry were to speak with Dad, which would almost certainly mean Fran would be driving the school car for a while. He was a very conscientious driver for a while.

I owe it to Gerry that I still recall the weather on my high school graduation day in May 1965. It was sunny and clear, and my classmates and I were driving around town in the afternoon with windows open. I remember that because a few of us had squirt guns and decided to have a shootout while cruising New England streets, shooting streams of water through open car windows. I was riding with Bob Freidt, and Gerry pulled us over. He apparently gave us some deference because it was our graduation day. Fortunately for me, Bob was issued the warning ticket; not me.

There were many teachers and events through my childhood years and college years that nudged me toward my eventual devotion to writing. The School Sisters of Notre Dame (SSND), based in Mankato, Minn., supplied the dedicated band of nuns who formed the majority of St. Mary's teaching staff. Many were raised in farming communities in Minnesota and other Midwest states, so they naturally seemed socially homogenous in New England. A few remained my friends for decades. My chemistry and physics teacher, Sister Gilmary (which means servant of Mary), is a southern Minnesota native. She imparted a joy in life and learning. She long ago reverted to her birth name, Pat Frost, spent decades as a missionary in central Africa. We still stay in touch.

One treasure early on was Sister Naomi, my fifth grade teacher. She was young, had a cheerful disposition generally and she liked playing softball, dodgeball and other athletic activities with kids in the school yard. She sometimes praised and encouraged the simple little things I wrote in English, history, science, etc.

One day, Sister Naomi put an array of magazine photographs on the board and asked us to write a poem about any one of them. I selected one with some cowhands sitting around a campfire and wrote this:

> *The cowboys were busy playing poker*
>
> *And forgot to watch their stoker.*

> *Then their fire went out*
>
> *And they began to pout and shout*
>
> *Because they couldn't cook their sauerkraut.*

She thought it was terribly funny and read it to the class. So I was the best fifth grade poet for a day. But I got support such as that from other teachers as well, and it encouraged me to try my hand often at writing.

It was also in my fifth grade that three other boys and I produced a sort of newsletter, a single-page gossip column. Our group and the newsletter were both called "The Fixers." Friend Ron Krebs or I typed news of which boys liked which girls, and vice versa, perhaps any news of a kiss being stolen, plus other rumors and allegations. When typed with the hardest strokes possible, a manual typewriter delivered an original and up to three carbon copies. We circulated them with requests to pass them on. Our effort survived for perhaps three or four issues. You have to start somewhere.

Through my St. Mary's High School years, George Ryan was one of the most positive influences on me. He coached varsity football and basketball and taught American history and current affairs. He was a tall, square-jawed and ruggedly handsome Irishman. He looked like a coach and was a good one. He and his wife had seven kids, and though his wife worked part time as well, I'm sure he needed every penny a Catholic school payroll provided.

Ryan had a great sense of humor off the field. Once when riding in his car to a football game, he was discussing a basketball topic with a couple of athletes in the front seat, and he posed the question: "What's a dribble?" Then, after a pause, provided the answer: "It's when you don't shake it before putting it back in your trousers." Of course, coming from our basketball coach, the joke was doubly funny. I believe it was Jim Schroeder who offered: "That is what I was thinking, but no way was I going to say it."

Ryan was well liked by most students, I think, and was certainly respected. His square jaw came into play on the football field and in the classroom, when he growled or barked what he expected of you. If you didn't get it, maybe growled it for you as well. Then grinned at you. Ryan's penalties for tardiness in the locker room and arriving late to football practice started with a minimum two laps around the football field before joining the practice. One afternoon, Ed Danks, a guard and a top player, came sprinting down the sharp embankment from the gymnasium to the field, plenty late to deserve penalty laps. But he had a dead song bird in his hand and reported to the coach how he was running so fast to get to practice that the poor bird was done in by his helmet. Ryan laughed and declared the excuse the most creative of the season. He assigned no penalty laps.

In our senior-year American civics class, Ryan often threw at us situations or events in U.S. history or current news and asked us to respond in class or in writing assignments. He opened his segment on civil rights with a long offensive monologue in which he distorted the history of black people and described a very subservient role for them in a white society. He said it was important to treat them kindly, but that they are only "trainable" to live successfully as servants of white people. Then he ended the class period with an assignment to write over the weekend about what he had said, about whether we agreed or disagreed and why.

I remember going, among other sources, to our home Encyclopedia Americana volumes to write my paper. I had already been coached on civil rights at home. In my paper, I quoted the U.S. Constitution and its applicable amendments, the encyclopedia's description of the Negroid race to argue, for example, that black people had no reported differences or deficiencies in size of brain or intelligence from Caucasians. I got an A on the paper, and our class got an earful about how important it is to know our civil rights and to be prepared to step up and defend them.

My time playing football and basketball under Ryan was foreshortened when, early in the 1963 season, classmate Dan Juelfs and I met head-on when charging down the field on a kickoff play. Dan planted his helmet into my collarbone, breaking it into chunks and splinters and ending my athletics for my junior year. Nonetheless, the team went on to win the Badlands Conference Football championship that year, and I gleaned a varsity letter and letterman's jacket for my brief efforts. In my senior year, since my skills in basketball were pretty thin, I worked out with the wrestling team for a couple of months. I even made varsity for one match. I was proud of that since my training in wrestling moves and holds was still very elementary, and St. Mary's had a very competitive team.

I did rejoin the football team as a very skinny tackle in the fall of 1964, and the team had a successful year. So did Hettinger High School's team, however, and the conference championship came down to beating Hettinger in our homecoming game, the last of the season. We were perhaps too confident of victory and likely thinking ahead to the homecoming dance. We found ourselves down 14-0 at halftime. Ryan went berserk, screaming at us at halftime that we were ready to blow off our whole season's work together. It was time to wake up and play like we knew how, he said. Everyone stepped up. Joe Roller, who went on to star in the Bison backfield at North Dakota State University, went crashing through the Hettinger line repeatedly. We seriously turned things around and won, 28-14.

This football memory concludes with Coach Ryan. We played football across town on New England's only lighted field, used by both New England High School and St. Mary's for football games, for summer baseball and softball league games, and more. We usually ran together with the coach or coaches to games and sometimes piled onto an open-boxed truck for the trip back to our dressing rooms after the game. So there were joyous chants and happy talk in the truck box about winning the game and conference title that night. As we were let off and walked past the front of the church, Ryan told us to go ahead to our dressing rooms, he turned to stop in at the church. But a friend and I dallied and peaked in the back doors of the church. Coach was kneeling in a back pew, and he was weeping.

Much of what happened behind the scenes at the parish and school administrative and staff, of course, passed over the heads of the pupils. In Ryan's case, I'll surely never know for certain all the reasons for his tears in church that evening. He had an alcoholism problem, a disease that complicates life and creates big troubles all by itself. Was Ryan just greatly relieved after working so hard to win a football coaching title, nearly losing it, and then snatching it back at the last minute from the jaws of defeat? Perhaps. Perhaps not. My next chapter is about his boss.

A Dark Character Called 'Big Dad'

For the Bismarck Catholic Diocese, St. Mary's parish was a target for Catholic schools expansion. Monsignor Aloysius Galowitsch was assigned as pastor of our parish and school superintendent in 1947 and led in raising funds and building the high school building plus a boys' dormitory. In 1953, when I was a first grader, Father Eugene La Meres was named to replace him, and he held the reins of the parish and school until eight years after I finished high school. To most of New England and to me, he was a dark character, known for his stern, unflinching glare. He ruled the parish and school and retained sole control of critical parish and school accounts. He delivered harsh sermons on faith, financial donations to the church, and devotion to Our Lady of Perpetual Help, the parish patron saint. His sermons touted sexual chastity a lot.

Eugene La Meres

La Meres raised funds successfully, and he led in building a new church, gymnasium, girls' dormitory and a convent during his tenure there. As noted earlier, School Sisters of Notre Dame formed the majority of St. Mary's teaching staff. He recruited athletes and other kids from hours away to board. That added to the parish's base of contributors and, thus, to income. The high school was an attractive choice for farm and ranch families who lived in remote locations in an era when many parts of North Dakota, South Dakota and Montana in that region still lacked decent roads, especially in winter.

La Meres was born in Golva, a small town in our area, and raised by a poor widow. He was smart and was valedictorian of his small Sentinel Butte High School senior class. He was able to complete his divinity and other degrees at top schools: St. John's University in Collegeville, Minn., and Marquette University in Milwaukee. I remember riding with him to attend a high school event in another city. He expressed the highest regard for advanced degrees, emphasizing the high social status of physicians, attorneys and priests: A status in which he, of course, placed himself. He saw ordination as his route to success and respect and, in his case as it turned out, great wealth.

But La Meres developed a double life. In his parish and town, he played the part of a fire-and-brimstone preacher. He seemed a loner and displayed a cold, somber facade. Many in New England, Catholic or not, called him "Big Dad" (accented on the Big), and he was feared by most adults and all kids, including youngsters of protestant faiths who attended New England Public School and over whom he had no authority.

La Meres outfitted himself with a Chrysler Imperial, a luxury sedan, which I understood he bought to mark his social status but also because he put on a lot of highway miles. One result of his choice in cars was St. Mary's High School pupils' ease in spotting his approach at a distance. I recall the recounting from about four high school boarder boys who were off campus without permission one afternoon. They found themselves down along the banks of the Cannonball River when they spotted the La Meres Chrysler coming down a sod road in their direction. They were so frightened that three of them jumped into the river with their clothes on to cross and escape La Meres. They hollered back to their friend, "come on, Frank, Big Dad is going to get you!" But, "I can't swim," Frank argued. They repeated their warning, and he jumped. Fortunately, the river was shallow enough for him to walk across.

La Meres' hard side was no secret, and George Ryan may have wept after winning that 1964 title because the pastor hired coaches and recruited athletes to win titles to boost the school's reputation and attract enrollments far and wide. So he may have feared dismissal if we had lost that game.

But there was more to it. La Meres had a horrific car accident in southern Minnesota in the summer of 1963, leaving him in critical condition, then bedridden for months. George's wife, Marianne, a registered nurse, attended to him during his long recovery. She was a pretty and vibrant redhead and one of the countless women whom La Meres enticed into his long line of physical hook-ups with women of many ages, including teenage girls. I heard rumors about La Meres and married women and other young lasses in those years, but didn't learn about Mr. Ryan and him until a few years later. However, Ryan likely knew full well about the pastor and his wife.

Many women related later to my family members and others how La Meres would counsel them as their pastor, then give them the pitch that he was lonely and needed physical contact and sexual fulfillment. He used that approach even with high school graduates who enrolled with the SSND nuns, and he would seduce them when driving them to or from the order's headquarters convent in Mankato.

Big Dad earned other labels, especially by those, including my parents, who were not cowed by his aggressive style and eventually uncovered some of his treachery and challenged him. "Skuz," many New Englanders called him. He had another weapon, my parents and their friends reported to me, for punishing church members who disagreed with him or for fending off those who later tried to have him removed. First, he had full control and knowledge of all parish and school accounts and apparently sole knowledge of critical ones. He was also very aggressive from the pulpit and otherwise in amassing pledges and donations. For example, he published parishioners' total financial contributions annually in the parish's Sunday bulletin. He pressed parishioners to tithe, which meant donating ten percent of their net income to the parish. His rule was that tithers' total giving would be listed simply as a "T" in the bulletin's annual list, but only if confirmed by submitting their annual IRS Form 1040s as confirmation of the ten percent share.

La Meres was never charged criminally with theft from his own parish. Such charges would be unlikely since he had total control of school and parish financial matters. The Catholic Diocese of Bismarck has authority over finances in its parishes, but the bishop at the time had his own personal situations and secrets that compromised his ability to call La Meres into account. So La Meres ran things as he wished. His fund raising included filling the gymnasium and school with people spending money at annual events such as the "fall festival" and school carnival. It became evident through his 20 years as St. Mary's pastor and school superintendent that his aggressive fund raising syphoned off funds for personal investments, although he many have also returned profits to the parish as well. The son of a poor widow arrived in New England as a young priest with no known income except a pastor's stipend, but left with countless millions of dollars.

In one incident, shortly after a St. Mary's fall festival in the early 1960s, a New England cop received a late night telephone call from police in Fort Collins, Colo., where La Meres owned at least one hotel during his New England tour. He had been stopped on a traffic violation, but things became complicated when police started checking out his car. The Fort Collins police wanted to know why a guy named Eugene La Meres would have bags full of cash in his trunk. When they described his Chrysler as well, the New England cop identified him as the local Catholic priest. "This is no priest," the Colorado policeman opined, noting that he had several young women in his car.

After La Meres' death in 1983, the U.S. Tax Court's findings of fact in settling unpaid tax issues in La Meres' estate stipulated these facts among others: Across the West – in California, New Mexico and Colorado – he owned ten hotels and 50 percent ownership in two more. Further, the Tax Court said, "In the years preceding his death, decedent traded between $20 million and $50 million worth of stock through five different brokers ... accumulated assets having a value of approximately $25 million net of liabilities." When inflating those 1980s sums into 21st Century dollars, that is a lot of money.

I will describe La Meres' mistreatment of his parishioners with just two brief examples. My parents and other New England residents related complaints from parishioners, including coaches, and ranchers with daughters in St. Mary's High School, who were victimized when the pastor used information in their Form 1040s to coerce them in various matter, and even to counter or restrain their complaints about his sexual aggression with their daughters and wives. One of my Dad's lifelong New England friends and the father of a large family, told him that he had to often awaken La Meres and get him out of an elder daughter's bedroom early in the morning before he left for his farm so the pastor wouldn't still be there when the rest of the family arose.

Another time, in the spring of 1963, I went into the church with my class during Lent to say the rosary with the entire high school. As

Maixner brothers served La Meres (back row) at mass and other events for years. Above, find me in front of his left arm; brother Rick, in the upper right corner.

we were ready to begin, La Meres ordered my brother Rick up the center aisle hand-in-hand with a girl he was dating. School rules forbade boys and girls from "going steady," and students were occasionally suspended for whatever La Meres decided was steady dating and what he observed or imagined two pupils' romantic relationship was. Rick and his girlfriend were made to complete the rosary together in the front pew. The incident was such an overt ridicule, never handed to any other students in such a public display. Perhaps it was retribution against my family because my parents did not hand in their 1040s to La Meres, though they did donate what it seemed to me at the time was a reasonable share of their income.

La Meres behavior deeply divided the people of St. Mary's parish for several years after I left New England. It is no surprise that my parents joined with a few other families and priests in appeals to the bishop of the diocese, trying to force his removal. My sister Darcy, for example, had to finish high school at a different Catholic school more than an hour from home because my parents' efforts made it impossible for her to continue at St. Mary's.

Today I see La Meres as a dark phenomenon who had a terrible impact on the parish and New England, but little negative impact on me directly. First, I wasn't aware of most of La Meres' worst antics while I was in school there. Plus the adults closest to me were mentally and morally sound and comfortable in their own skins and with their faith. I expect the La Meres experience helped me more clearly separate Christians, a bunch of sinners, from a faith that calls us to be less so.

Hence, I left high school with a positive attitude overall about Catholicism and viewed life as a priest or nun as admirable. In fact, in my senior year I enrolled in the Catholic seminary at St. Mary's College in Winona, Minn. I spent only my freshman year there, but it was a great year, because seminaries were focused much more than American Catholic parishes at the time on what was becoming a more inclusive and modern approach to Christianity.

The North Coast Limited was taken by all rail travelers in our area until Amtrak took over in 1971. (Photo by Doug Wingfield, Lethbridge, Alberta)

Trips & Vacations

I enjoyed a lot of trips through my childhood years either with the family or by myself to visit friends or relatives, or to participate in school events. As is usual in most families, my parents' leash lengthened as I got older. I recall getting to use the well in the North Dakota Senate chamber to argue my position on model legislation as part of a statewide Student Congress competition. The nun advising us little lawmakers thought that the way I was snapping my clipboard at my fellow senators to emphasize my points was kind of funny.

By the time I hit summer 1964, after my junior year, I went by Northern Pacific's passenger train, called the *North Coast Limited* (see https://goo.gl/cEcPon online) to Fargo to attend a 4-H leadership conference at North Dakota State University. Tracy Walth, a classmate, also went, and we were able to play hooky one afternoon and run around in downtown Fargo, watch an Elvis Presley movie (*Viva Las Vegas*) and grab a city bus back to campus in the early evening. It was a thrill being footloose in the largest city that I had ever visited.

North Coast Limited trips were a fun and adventurous exception to my usual seat in the Maixner station wagon for long trips and vacations. I recall my Aunt Marie Wolff dropping Joe and me off at the Bismarck passenger depot and my parents greeting us at the Dickinson depot when we were perhaps nine or ten years old.

Winona, which is where I was enrolled in the seminary for a year, is on Minnesota's eastern border, and I commuted across that state and most of North Dakota a couple of times with my seminary friends, playing cards and cribbage and eating snacks in the club cars. The North Coast Limited operated from Seattle to Chicago. It had an historically long run, from 1900 until Amtrak took over rail passenger service on that route in 1971 and renamed the train as the North Coast Hiawatha. It had domed lounges on some cars, plus diner and sleeper cars. It was among the best passenger trains on America's rails.

From an early age, we took family day trips to fish at Cedar Lake, a shallow reservoir several miles south of the farm that silted in extensively in later decades. We drove to Hamman Dam, northwest of Amidon, to fish as well. We water skied there a couple of times with the Narums, who had a modest craft with a 25-horsepower outboard engine. That is where the older Maixner siblings first skied. Family outings were typically to movies in New England or Dickinson, to attend a rodeo, circus or other event in Dickinson.

A benefit rodeo, called the Champions Ride (see hotrnd.com/champions-ride-rodeo online), has been held each August for more than 60 years at Home on the Range, a Catholic-affiliated ranch home that helps troubled youth and families. The event was

We cut Christmas trees occasionally in public areas of the nearby badlands.

more than an hour's drive west of our farm, on the far side of the North Dakota Badlands and Theodore Roosevelt National Park. Thus, the rodeo was a full day's excursion that began with the rear of the station wagon stocked with blankets, jackets, coolers full of food and soft drinks. TR National Park was a favorite place to visit in warm months, but we also drove into nearby public lands near the park to harvest a Christmas tree in December of some years.

Considering that we were still about a decade away from the interstate highway system in western North Dakota, and a drive to Bismarck was on two-lane highways, we did well to make fairly frequent weekend or holiday trips to Bismarck to visit my Steckman grandparents and the rest of Mom's family there.

Grandpa Steckman occasionally took Joe and I and other siblings to fish at Sweet Briar Lake, Apple Creek and Crown Butte Dam, all near Bismarck. One fishing trip had Joe and I went with Grandpa and Grandma Steckman for a day at Lake Sakakawea just as the reservoir was forming. Garrison Dam was built by the U.S. Army Corps of Engineers in 1947 to 1953, and the water behind it, Lake Sakakawea, was filled to minimum operating level in 1955, according to the U.S. Army Corps of Engineers, who built and maintain the dam and facilities.

I remember our fishing trip with the Steckmans when reservoir was still filling or nearly filled. Garrison created one of the world's largest man-made reservoirs, so it was a very big deal in North Dakota. Several miles across, Sakakawea was by far the biggest expanse of water I had seen at my eight or nine years of life. One very miserable aspect of the Garrison project: It flooded the Mandan, Hidatsa and Arikara Indians' lowlands, where they lived and farmed along the Missouri River. The project forced them to live on higher, less productive land where winter winds are harsher.

Farms with livestock tend to keep family vacations brief. But they were expanded as the Maixner kids matured and as my parents got the farm well enough established to pay for trips along with hired hands to do chores while we were away. Family vacations tended to be back-to-nature excursions. We drove to Yellowstone National Park one year, for example, and the South Dakota Black Hills another year. When I was a high school freshman, we took a week to drive through Montana to southern Idaho to attend my brother Bill's wedding. His bride, Judy Frew, became my first sibling in-law. Her sister, Mary Michal, was my age, and we became life-long pals.

Dad liked fishing as well as a break from farming, and he instigated our annual fishing trips into Canada in 1961. That was shortly after Bill, the oldest brother, had tried college briefly in Helena, Mont., then joined the Air Force. So all of us, except Bill, got in on at least a couple of those Canadian vacations. They were always at the end of May or early June, and for a good reason. Grain and other field crops in southwestern North Dakota are planted in April and May. Also, most of the steers and heifers that had been fed through the winter and spring in the feedlot had been sold off as yearlings by June, or they were heifers being added to the cow herd in the pasture. So, except for milking the cows, picking eggs and feeding the chickens, there were few immediate labor needs, allowing a window of a week before the first cuttings of hay crops had to begin. In that lull, we left for lakes in Saskatchewan or Manitoba to fish walleye pike, northern pike and other game fish. The Maixner kids all fished, but enjoyed it in varied degrees. As young adults, some siblings and our families continued to join up with my parents for Canadian fishing vacations.

Mom was not a water person. She didn't fish, and since she didn't swim either, she didn't get into boats. Yet she enjoyed the trips as much as any of us. We cleaned our catch, and she fried fish and managed the whole food supply and menu for her large troupe. She read books, played cards and other games with us in our cabin and so forth. Rick recalls that Mom forgot to bring flour on one of the first such trips. But she did bring plenty of pancake flour, so that was used instead to bread the fresh fillets, and became a traditional Maixner way of frying fish.

Back at the Flying M, we had weekend and holiday visits back and forth with families of close friends in the New England and Amidon areas who had several kids in a similar span of ages. That began with the Jacobs cousins and included the families of Hugh and Millie Brentrup, Ken and Carrie Narum, Leo "Red" and Betty Gardner, Frank and Cecelia Roller and others. I also stayed overnight or a few days occasionally with those families and others: for example, on a nearby farm with Ron Schmitt, one of my first close friends.

Regular diversions with friends in New England included the swimming pool, basketball, baseball and softball, bowling at the lanes that opened when I was in junior high, or just hanging out at the bowling alley. But we also ranged out of town occasionally. For example, to fish at Karey Dam, a small reservoir nearby on the Cannonball River, or to hike from our farmstead to the East Rainy with a tent and other gear and food for a night of camping near the spring there. Or sometimes farther afield: Cal Steiner and I went to Catholic Boys Camp on Lake Metigoshe when I was about 12 years old. The lake is next to the Manitoba border, and so my first visit to a foreign country was an afternoon hike along a graveled backroad into Canada.

From about eighth grade on through high school, a favorite was going home for a weekend with Dick Knopp, whose parents ran a ranch about an hour's drive from New England in a remote spot that includes some of the most rugged and unusually pretty scenery of the North Dakota Badlands. We hunted, watched television and so forth. The banter with Dick's older sisters on the long drive home and during the weekend offered clues to what was in the heads of older teenage girls, who seemed an exotic species at the time. Weekends at Knopps included regular cattle care chores like those on our farm, but also insight into how two cattle operations vary in animal husbandry, nutrition and so forth. Our farm had a couple of bulls to breed the herd of cows, for example, but Richard Knopp Sr. sold Hereford bulls as breeding stock, which meant that about a third of the herd were bulls. Feeding and moving through a herd of bulls required a lot more caution than around our cattle, even though Herefords are known as an even-tempered breed.

Knopps were about an hour's drive nearer than our farm was to the lowlands along the Yellowstone River, where farms raised sugar beets and sold leftover beet pulp as a cattle feed component. So visiting Knopps was, for example, my introduction to beet pulp as cattle feed. Also, the early 1960s were a few years before big round hay bales became popular on farms. We stacked most of our hay, then lifted chunks of it from a haystack with tractor-mounted hydraulic forks (like a big set of kitchen tongs) and dumped the hay into feed bunks, or took it with the tractor to where our cows were on the farmstead and dumped it there. The Knopps bailed most of their hay, so they loaded bales onto a truck to distribute them, and gave cattle in the pasture compressed biscuits of ground grain, "feed cake," in winter months.

One weekend with Dick featured a near-disaster that no farm boy would forget. Dick had the use of his parents' new Pontiac to see a basketball game or other event in Beach, a small town on the west edge of North Dakota. Two of Dick's best friends joined him, and the four of us cruised around Beach's main routes. One of his pals contributed a pint of gin to the get-together, and the bottle was open and on the floor of the rear seat when a local police officer pulled Dick over for accelerating too fast out of a turn (or for being a kid driver with a hot car perhaps). Anyway, no one owned up to owning the bottle, which I believe we claimed just happened to be left in the car.

To resolve the matter, the cop took us to the Golden Valley County sheriff's office, where the sheriff put us in jail for a while to help us clarify our story. When we were told that one good way of resolving the problem was to call our parents to pick us up (mine were a two-hour drive away), I believe we produced answers that the cops preferred. They let us go home without the bottle after a couple of hours as jailbirds. I was more than a little relieved they did not call my parents.

Flying M family

In 1966, then nearly all grown up: in front, Darcy, parents Laura and Dick, Laura Lu; in back, Ed, Bill, Joel, Rick, and twins Fran and Frank

Made in the USA
Columbia, SC
10 June 2019